WEIGHTS, MONEY AND OTHER MEASURES
USED BY OUR ANCESTORS

Colin R Chapman

FIRST EDITION

Originally published in 1995 as part of the
Chapmans Records Cameos Series by
Lochin Publishing, 6 Holywell Road, Dursley,
Gloucestershire GL11 5RS, England

Published in the U.S.A., 1996, by
arrangement with Lochin Publishing
by Genealogical Publishing Co., Inc.
1001 N. Calvert Street, Baltimore, MD 21202

Reprinted with minor alterations, 1997

The original English edition was published under the
title *How Heavy, How Much and How Long? Weights, Money
and Other Measures Used by Our Ancestors*. The American
edition uses only the subtitle of the English edition.

Library of Congress Catalogue Card Number 95-81652
International Standard Book Number 0-8063-1501-6
Made in the United States of America

The cover illustration is adapted by Nick Ind from Leonardo
da Vinci's pen drawing in the first chapter of the third book of
Vitruvius. The original is 343 x 245 mm, catalogued as No.
228 in the Accademia in Venice, Italy. Other illustrations in
this Cameo are also by Nick Ind.

Table of Contents

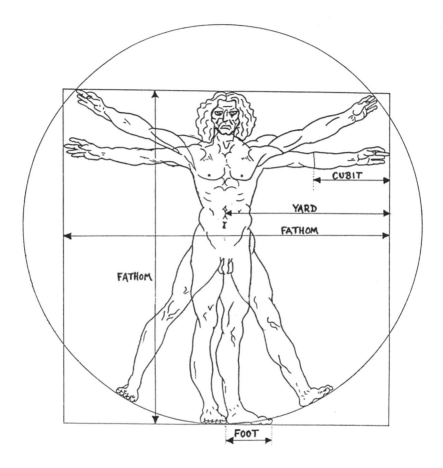

Frontispiece. Leonardo da Vinci's Vitruvian Man - see Chapter 2.

Preface

I can still remember clutching my grandmother's hand as a small child in the baker's shop and seeing her delight, when buying a dozen bread rolls, at receiving 13 of them from the ruddy-faced proprietor in his tall, crumpled white hat. I also recall living in the tropics and being told a colleague would be with me in a couple of hours, only to find he arrived over five hours later; I then realised that a couple does not universally indicate two - and possibly other units of measurement do not mean the same to everyone.

While exploring the intrigues of the manorial system I was enraptured by area measurements such as oxgangs and hides. My work on early population listings had revealed virgates and farthingales to me. My father had an allotment during the Second World War that was 10 rods in area - or was it poles or perches? - they had long fascinated me. At school we learned by rote the idiosyncrasies of gills, pecks and bushels as measures of capacity; and the tables of mass and weight with drams, ounces, stones, quarters, hundredweights and tons had been drummed into our minds so firmly that even now I can repeat them effortlessly.

Coins and tradesmen's tokens appeal to any youth and I was no exception, handling Victorian farthings and silver threepenny pieces, half-crowns and florins and copper Welsh mine tokens. I looked longingly at museum collections of golden guineas, and half, third and quarter-guineas with nobles and sovereigns, even gold crowns and silver pennies. The introduction in 1971 of decimal money filled some of us with horror as we believed the very fabric of British society was crumbling in our pockets. The ease of multiplying or dividing everything by ten did little to appease my own sorrow at the demise of such lovely names as the groat, the farthing and the tanner.

My involvement in science exposed me to metric systems from CGS, MKS and MKSA to SI units, changing in definition while my engineering career developed. In 1987 when visiting what was then East Berlin, I discovered the statue of Theodor Mommsen on the forecourt of Humboldt University; he was, and still is, one of my 19th Century heroes who had suggested the origins of Roman numerals. Returning to Humboldt University during 1994, accompanied by the illustrator of this book, I renewed my reverence for Mommsen who was still sitting majestically outside that great academy of learning.

At one stage in my life I enjoyed living in a former public house. When investigating its history I came across references to earthenware crinzes, wooden mazers, leather piggins, pewter quaiches and glass rummers - all mugs and drinking vessels that your ancestors or mine may have held to their parched lips as they slaked their thirsts generations ago. How much they drank and its cost was the subject of much agreeable research. I am able to share some of the results of that research with you in the following pages.

In preparing this material two measurements initially caused me particular problems: the styke or stick and the sheaf or chief. The former was most confusingly used to indicate both a number of eels and also as an alternative for ells in measuring the length of cloth. The latter is spelled variously as chief, chef, sheaf, shave and shive to indicate pieces or slices of cloth and of iron and thatching materials such as straw and reeds. In the tables which follow, I have chosen to allocate chief to cloth and sheaf to iron and thatching materials.

I was given a copy of *Nuttall's Table Book* in about 1950 (it cost 4d) and have retained my 1951 *Schoolboy's Pocket Book*. Perhaps it is these, or maybe other catalysts, that prompted me to collect together some past, and a few present, units of length and area, volume and capacity, mass and weight, currency and metric equivalents, before they are lost forever. It is with these as my base that I have prepared this Cameo for us all to enjoy a selection of measurements used by our ancestors and relate them to our own experiences. Scales of temperature and some specialized mechanical measures, such as those for screw threads, have been deliberately omitted.

It was my original intention to provide a chapter on time measurement from millenia to seconds, including calendars, regnal years, sporting and quarterly seasons, Christian Festivals and nautical watches. However, space did not permit these topics to be included here; they form the subject of a separate Cameo.

I am extremely grateful to Dr R D Connor, Professor of Physics and Dean Emeritus of the Faculty of Science at the University of Manitoba, Winnipeg (his own book [ref. 8] is the authoritative work), for meticulously reading a draft of this Cameo and offering many improvements. Any errors are my responsibility.

COLIN R CHAPMAN.

"He is a chapman, the balances of deceit are in his hand". Hosea Ch 12, v 7.

Introduction

The chapters that follow are for readers who come across unfamiliar units of weight and other measurement when reading books and documents from years gone by. They will also prove helpful for word-puzzle addicts or anyone with a passion for obscure and unusual facts. They may even bridge a generation gap or two by helping to elucidate more of the lives of our forebears. A handy glossary of weights and other measures is provided in a series of tables enabling readers to readily see relationships between various units. Cross references are provided where relevant. The chapter titles speak for themselves, but for those who are unsure if a particular measurement indicates a number, a coin or a capacity etc, the index provides easy access to the tables. It is, therefore, the ideal companion to keep by one's side when perusing wills, inventories and accounts, browsing through old diaries and journals, or merely idling away a few moments between the more demanding periods of the day.

Perhaps this book should be entitled Metrology, the accurate measurement of mass and length and their derivations, area and volume etc; but some readers would have passed it by, believing it to be connected with the weather. Mensuration may have attracted others, but we shall not get involved here with a mathematical treatment (geometry, trigonometry and calculus) of lengths, areas and volumes. Rather we shall identify fundamental quantities of length, mass and account to see, in tabular form, how these were used as a basis for areas and capacities and how they and other quantities have changed over the centuries.

It is tempting in a work of this nature to include units of measurement or value simply for the quaintness of their names such as the gait, used almost exclusively in Northamptonshire to indicate 2 buckets of water, or the waw, which comprised 40 bundles of glass. However, the average reader will meet these and many similar local affixes so rarely that recourse to a voluminous and comprehensive dictionary will be more appropriate to reveal their meaning and origin, than swelling the pages of this compact working manual with such localized terms.

Pheidon, King of Argos (about 7th Century BC) in Peloponnesus in ancient Greece caused a standard weight (a drachma) to be used; the values he had were certainly in place when Solon conducted his major reforms in Athens soon after 600 BC. Pheidon is said also to have initiated the stamping of gold and silver coins and before his time iron rods or spits had been used as currency, a bundle of such rods being also used as a weight. The Jews, however, historically believed that Cain had introduced weights and measures (some Biblical measurements are listed in Chapters 2, 3 and 4), while the Egyptians ascribed their origin to Thoth, their god of wisdom and letters.

Many of the ancient measures were based on the natural proportions of an average human body, a fundamental unit, the digit, being the breadth of the centre portion of the first joint of the forefinger. A fathom is the distance between the ends of the tips of the middle fingers of a man's outstretched arms, about equal to his height. The Vitruvian man drawn by Leonardo da Vinci to demonstrate the body's proportions, simplified on the cover of this Cameo and annotated in the frontispiece, illustrates this. Other body measures are described in Chapter 2. A mile is a modern version of the Old English word 'mil', taken from the Latin 'milia passuum', being 1000 strides. In addition to the human body, and because our ancestors derived their livelihoods from the land and crops, grain was also used as a fundamental measure: three barleycorns placed end to end measured one inch and 24 barleycorn grains weighed a pennyweight.

But, regardless of Leonardo's extensive research, no two forefingers are the same size and no two individuals are the same height or cover the same distance when taking 1000 strides, and even barleycorns are not all equal; hence these measures were by no means consistent or standardized. This did not appear to worry our distant ancestors unduly and in the British Isles it took a great number of royal proclamations and Acts of Parliament, spread over many hundred years, to achieve national standards. And then in the twentieth century many of the quaint and romantic, but by then standardized, British weights, lengths, other measures and currency were tossed aside as metrication and decimalisation crept into the daily lives of the British peoples.

There was so much legislation enacted in attempts to bring standardization to British weights and other measures that it would be impossible to describe or even list every national and local Act and Decree here. The forerunners of inspectors of weights and measures such as ballast assessors, bread weighers, butter searchers, clerks of markets, coal weighers, corn measurers, inspectors of fish and flesh, leather searchers and wool weighers were appointed by manorial courts and municipal authorities from the earliest times to encourage fair and consistent trading standards. As early as 972 King Edgar introduced a law under which a standard measure was to be kept at Winchester. Around the time of the Domesday Survey (1086) William I required all weights and measures to be authenticated with the Royal Seal and in 1197 Richard I's Assize of Measures enabled every borough to appoint custodians of approved local copies of standard weights and measures, provided by the sheriffs of London.

The Magna Carta, sealed by King John in 1215, and reiterated by Henry III in 1225, included a chapter requiring one measure for wine, one for ale and one for corn and laid down a standard width for certain cloths. In 1266 the Assize of Bread and Ale stipulated standard weights and measures for these essential commodities and soon afterwards in *Compositio Ulnarum et Perticarum*, standards were established for linear and area measures. At the beginning of the 14th Century, Edward I repeated the linear and area standards, quoted values for the wine gallon and the London bushel and (in 1305) amalgamated body and agricultural measurements in an Ordinance for Measuring Land, which fixed the area of an acre at 160 square perches. Edward II and Edward III restated previous requirements of standard weights and measures; lengths of ray and coloured cloths were standardized and in 1351 (and in several later Statutes of Edward III) auncel balances (see Chapter 5) were banned. The 1357 Statute of Westminster required merchants to have their weights and balances tested by the county sheriffs, although in 1360 the Justices were made responsible for local copies of Crown standards. Some standard weights from this time of 91, 56, 28, 14 and 7 pounds, have survived and are in Winchester Museum, England.

During Richard II's reign, the capacities of containers of imported wine were required to be scrutinised and the duties of the Clerks of the Market were laid down; standard measures for cloths were abandoned, although reinstated, abolished and reinstated again under Henry IV. Coal measures were standardized by Henry V in 1421, while two years later, under Henry VI, the varying capacities of barrels, hogsheads, tertians, pipes and tuns were identified for different goods. Henry VI also standardized the value of cheese measures (see Table 5.13), reminded merchants that auncels were forbidden, and gave the Justices extra responsibilities for standards. During the reign of Edward IV, cloth lengths were to be measured by the ell, the sizes of firewood faggots and billets were standardized (Table 4.4) by the Assize of Fuel, and eel and herring barrel capacities were standardized (Table 4.6).

Under Henry VII national standard weights and measures were distributed to an identified town in each of the 43 counties where locally appointed officials were to ensure adherence to these. Henry VIII confirmed that situation and during his reign the Tower Pound was abolished (see Chapter 5), ale and beer vessel capacities were standardized, and from 1532 to 1536 butchers were required to sell meat by weight. Under Edward VI and Mary I earlier Acts regarding fuel and cloth measures were reinforced. In 1581 Elizabeth I required honey measures to conform to those for wine, while in 1588 she organized the manufacture of new physical standards for the yard and ell and a series of Troy weights from 256 to ⅛ ounces and a series of Avoirdupois weights from 56 pounds to 1 dram. In 1601 capacity measures of 1 bushel, 1 gallon, 1 quart and 1 pint were also manufactured. All these, which remained the nation's primary standards until 1826, are now in the Science Museum, South Kensington, London.

The duties of the Clerks of the Market were clarified in 1640 under Charles I and, on his Restoration in 1660, Charles II extended Henry VIII's ale and beer vessel standards; the weight standards of butter, coal and salt were regulated in 1662 and 1670. An Act in 1681 reviewed all weights and measures. During the reigns of William III and of Anne the dimensions of the Winchester barrel were standardized (in 1701), the wine gallon was fixed at 231 cubic inches (in 1706), woollen cloths measures were standardized for Yorkshire (in 1708), the 1266 Assize of Bread was repealed (in 1709) but new regulations were introduced and in 1713 the coal bushel was standardized. Scottish cloth sizes were regulated in 1719 under George I, and under George II the selling of coal by the sack was controlled by Acts of 1730 and 1758. In 1795 George III established procedures to be followed by county inspectors and in 1803 the capacities of ale and beer barrels were unified (see Table 4.7).

The 1824 Weights and Measures Act, which became effective on 1 January 1826, caused the 1588 standards to be replaced by new Imperial standards. The new Imperial standard yard, and the Troy pound, both in brass, were held at the House of Commons. The Avoirdupois pound from this date was to be a secondary standard made by comparison with the Troy standard and the Imperial standard gallon was to be the measure for all fluids and dry goods, containing 10 Avoirdupois pounds of distilled water at 62°F. The bushel was to contain 80 Avoirdupois pounds of water. Authenticated copies were made for national distribution and purchased by Justices of the Peace for local use throughout the country.

Disastrously the new primary standards were destroyed in a fire that consumed both Houses of Parliament in 1834. But this event did give the committee set up to replace the standard measures a unique opportunity to incorporate the latest scientific expertise and practices. Accordingly an 1855 Act declared the Avoirdupois pound to be the standard, based on a pound weight made of platinum and dated 1844, leaving the other measures as in the 1824 Act; the new yard was manufactured in bronze and dated 1845. The standards were deposited with the Exchequer in 1853 but transferred to the Board of Trade in 1866.

However, another committee had reported in 1862 that there were still in use ten systems of weights (having 14 different stone weights alone), three different fathoms (6 feet for warships, 5½ feet for merchantships and 5 feet for fishing vessels) and twenty different bushels for capacity. The 1878 Act tidied up many of these variant measures and abolished the Troy pound, retaining the Troy ounce only for bullion and precious stones. This was reinforced in 1893 and then in 1897 an Act made provision for the introduction of metric weights and measures, which were gradually and reluctantly acknowledged (but not entirely accepted) by the British public during the latter half of the 20th Century.

The 1963 Weights and Measures Act drove a major nail into the coffin of Imperial measures by defining a yard as 0.9144 metre exactly, an Avoirdupois pound as 0.45359237 kilogram exactly and a gallon as 4.545964591 litres; the rod, pole, perch, square rod, bushel, peck and pennyweight were to be abolished from 31 January 1969, after when Apothecaries' Measures were to be phased out. But most of these measures refused to leave the British scene quietly and hence the 1976 Weights and Measures Act was needed to restate the abolition of the bushel, peck, pennyweight and Apothecaries' Measures. By the 1976 Act drachms, minims, scruples, Apothecaries' ounces and like measures should have been banished for ever but tradition is difficult to eradicate in Britain.

In desperation the government introduced a further Weights and Measures Act in 1985, abolishing for purposes of trading, the linear measures of furlong and chain, the area measures of square inch, rood and square mile, the solid measures of cubic inch, cubit foot and cubic yard, the Apothecaries' fluid scruple, drachm and ounce and, yet again, the bushel and peck and also the mass and weights of grain, pennyweight, stone, quarter, hundredweight, cental, ton and metric ton. The yard, mile, square foot, gallon, Avoirdupois pound and ounce and Troy ounce (albeit subdivided metrically) somehow escaped extinction by this Act. Nevertheless, as with the introduction of decimal currency, many thought the end of the world was nigh, but as expressed most aptly in the Bible: "Divers weights and divers measures, both of them are alike abomination to the Lord" (Proverbs Ch 20, v 10).

The saga is obviously not yet complete in the British Isles with a few Imperial and even more ancient measures lingering on. At the time of writing, petrol is sold in litres while milk bottles contain a pint; Northampton is 90 miles from Gloucester but I am 1.7 metres tall; I can buy a pound of carrots but have to purchase 500 grams of sugar. The future of individual European countries retaining their separate currencies is under debate, but clocks and watches continue to be manufactured around the world bearing Arabic or Roman numerals. Whilst our thinking on these matters continues to remain inconsistent, the following chapters will prove useful in interpreting some of the inconsistencies.

For details on derivations of many of the English weights and measures (though not money) referred to in the following tables, readers should consult Ronald Zupko's *Dictionary* [ref. 30]; but for a thoroughly academic exposition on the entire subject of English weights and measures, Robin Connor's book [ref. 8] is the definitive work. For measures used particularly in Scotland, Ireland, Wales and some "British Dominions", see Nicholson [ref. 22]; (the actual areas mentioned are the Channel Islands, Cape Colony - South Africa - India, Burma and Straits, Canada and Mauritius). Some of the values quoted from *Chronology* [ref. 27] should be interpreted in the knowledge that it was not a scientific treatise.

The sources from which the data shown in the tables have been derived are identified, where appropriate, at the top right-hand side of each table, by the numbers allocated in References and Bibliography on page 85.

For those readers who wish to translate monetary denominations into the vulgar tongue, a handy chart is provided on the inside of the back cover. Vulgar names are given in alphabetical order beside each denomination, arranged by class in decreasing value. The names included have been used by "crooks, criminals, racketeers, beggars and tramps, convicts, the commercial underworld" and others, perhaps your ancestors, over several centuries. To avoid confusion, these names, and others used throughout the explanatory text at the commencement of each chapter, have not been included in the Index to the Tables.

1. General Numeration

The Greeks, Romans and Hebrews experienced considerable numeration problems having no symbols to use as working numerals. Their systems of ascribing letters were really suitable only for recording numerals, making calculations virtually impossible; thus for numerical working they used an abacus on which multiplication was easy, although division was quite cumbersome and inaccurate. In 1850 Theodor Mommsen suggested that Roman numerals were derived from finger positions. One finger represents I, a hand of five fingers represents V, and two fives, one inverted, create X for 10. If ten groups of five, fifty, are represented by L, two fifties, one inverted similarly to the fives, create L or C for 100. The Roman lack of a connection between I, V, X, L, C, D and M, and the total lack of a symbol for zero, with no easy method of indicating ten times, created untold difficulties. The practice of writing lines over or beside Roman numerals (Table 1.2) was not used by the Romans; this was conceived considerably after the fall of the Roman Empire in the mediaeval period by scholars struggling to use Roman numerals to indicate large numbers.

It was not until the so-called Arabic numerals (actually a Hindu concept brought from India by the Persians) were adopted, with the wonderful notion of a zero symbol, that numeracy became a language by which builders, accountants and mathematicians could communicate. The crusaders, visiting the Middle East, brought Arabic numerals to western Europe where they entered common usage from the 14th Century.

Numbers are either *proper* (a count) or *common* (an estimate), depending on whether they represent an exact count (such as 16 great-grandparents) or an estimate (such as being 6 feet tall); more precise measurement cannot provide 15.8 or 16.5 great-grandparents, but may indicate a height of 5 feet 11¾ inches. The Chinese *Book of the Permutations* (c1100 BC) regarded odd numbers 1, 3, 5 etc as masculine with even numbers 2, 4, 6 etc being perfectly divisible by two, as feminine. The ideal combination of numerals was a union or marrying of odd and even numerals to give the perfect sequence 1, 2, 3, 4, 5, 6 etc.

Certain commodities were in such constant use that special units were applied to indicate standard quantities, such as a brace of pheasants, a dozen eggs, a stoke of trenchers, a load of bricks, a kiver of thatching straw, a ream of paper, a warp of fish, a rope of onions or a binne of skins. All these and many other tales (quantities), including numerals formerly used to count sheep, are given in the following tables, concluding with definitions of both American and British millions and the prefixes used for multiples of the power of ten.

Table 1.1 Commercial Numbers   [37, 40, 41]

1 brace (a pair)	=	2 items
1 dozen	=	12 items
1 long (baker's) dozen	=	13 items
1 gross	=	12 dozen (144 items)
1 long gross	=	156 items
1 score	=	20 items
1 common hundred	=	5 score (100 items)
1 long * or great hundred	=	6 score (120 items)
1 hundred	=	4 quarters
1 quarter	=	80 deals

* until the 16th Century usually referred to solely as a hundred.

Table 1.2a Roman Numerals - Fundamental Symbols   [46]

Fundamental Numerals	Multiples of Numerals
1 = I or i	
5 = V or v	$5,000 = \overline{V}$ *
10 = X or x	$10,000 = \overline{X}$
50 = L or l	$50,000 = \overline{L}$
100 = C or c	$100,000 = \overline{C}$
500 = D †	$500,000 = \overline{D}$
1000 = M †	$1,000,000 = \overline{M}$

* the use of — over a symbol was introduced in the mediaeval period to indicate a multiplication of 1000. Using | | around a symbol indicated a multiplication of 100,000; eg |X| (or $|\overline{X}|$) is 1,000,000.

† see note ‡ to Table 1.2b.

Table 1.2b Roman Numerals - Compound Symbols   [19]

1 = I	6 = VI	11 = XI	16 = XVI
2 = II	7 = VII	12 = XII	17 = XVII
3 = III	8 = VIII	13 = XIII	18 = XVIII
4 = IV *	9 = IX	14 = XIV	19 = XIX
5 = V	10 = X	15 = XV	20 = XX
28 = XXVIII	200 = CC	2,000 = MM	
30 = XXX	300 = CCC	3,000 = MMM	
40 = XL	400 = CD †	4,000 = $M\overline{V}$	
50 = L	500 = D ‡	5,000 = $\overline{V}$	
60 = LX	600 = DC	6,000 = $\overline{V}M$	
70 = LXX	700 = DCC	7,000 = $\overline{V}MM$	
80 = LXXX	800 = DCCC	8,000 = $\overline{V}MMM$	
90 = XC	900 = CM	9,000 = $M\overline{X}$	
100 = C	1,000 = M	10,000 = $\overline{X}$	
Year 1538 = MDXXXVIII			
Year 1851 = MDCCCLI			
Year 1939 = MCMXXXIX			

Notes:

When more than one lower case i is used in a compound number, the last numeral one appears as j; eg, 3 = iij, 28 = xxviij, 42 = xlij.

* sometimes written as IIII (or iiij).

† sometimes written as CCCC.

‡ this could be derived from IƆ, although the apostrophus (Ɔ) was normally used after IƆ to indicate a multiplication of ten; in other words IƆ is 500, IƆƆ is 5000, IƆƆƆ is 50,000 etc. Using the apostrophus also enabled a number to be doubled by adding the same number of Cs at the front of the number as there were Ɔs in the number; in other words IƆ is 500, CIƆ is 1000, CCIƆƆ is 10,000. In fact, it has been argued that M, the symbol for 1000 in Tables 1.2a and 1.2b is derived from CIƆ, in the same way that D is derived from IƆ.

Table 1.3   *Quantities of Building Materials*   [14]

Material	Term	Number
Bricks	a load	500
Tiles	a load	1000
Nails, Tacks	an hundred	6 score
	a sum	10,000
Timber	100 deals	120 pieces

See also Tables 4.2 and 4.3.

Table 1.4   *Quantities of Thatching Materials*   [14]

1 kiver *	=	12 sheaves †
1 thrave	=	2 kivers ‡

* also termed a stook.
† also termed boltings, bundles and trusses.
‡ by the 19th Century.
In Scotland in 1523, 1 thrave = 4 sheaves.
see also Table 5.11.

Table 1.5   *Quantities of Iron*   [14]

1 sheaf	=	30 gads *
1 burden	=	12 sheaves

* or billets, also termed gaddy, garb and bar.
In Scotland in the 13th Century 1 sheaf = 16 gads.

Table 1.6   *Quantities of Trenchers* *   [14]

1 stoke	=	60 pieces

* wooden table-ware (platters, dishes etc).

Table 1.7 *Quantities of Paper & Parchment* [14, 40, 42, 45]

Writing Paper	Printing Paper
1 quire = 24 sheets	1 ream = 516 * sheets
1 ream = 20 quires	1 bundle = 2 reams
1 ream = 480 sheets	1 bale = 5 bundles
1 mille = 1000 sheets	

* sometimes 500 sheets.

For sizes of paper see Tables 3.8 and 3.9.

One parchment roll comprised 5 dozen (60) skins.

Table 1.8 *Quantities of Fish* [14, 37, 42]

1 hand	=	2 fish
1 warp	=	4 fish
1 long hundred	=	33 warps (132 fish)
10 hundred	=	1320 fish
1 maze *	=	5 long hundreds
1 last	=	13,200 fish
1 glean herrings	=	25 fish
1 rees herrings	=	15 gleans
1 cran	=	37½ Imperial gallons †
1 barrel	=	26¾ Imperial gallons †
1 quintal ‡	=	112 pounds

Note: a long hundred of salt fish is 120 fish; Doggerbank fishermen calculate 124 to the long hundred; hence the last (100 long hundreds) can vary.

• used on West Coast of British Isles, Isle of Man and Ireland.

† this varies for salmon to 35 Imperial gallons; see also Table 4.6.

‡ a measure later used in the metric system to indicate 100 kilograms.

Table 1.9 *Quantities of Eels*   [14]

1 stick	=	25 eels
1 gwyde *	=	10 sticks

* also termed a bind, but this could be 33 eels.

Table 1.10 *Quantities of Onions & Garlic*   [14]

1 rope	=	15 heads
1 hundred	=	15 ropes
	=	225 onions/garlic

Table 1.11 *Quantities of Hides*   [14]

1 dicker	=	10 hides
1 last	=	20 dickers *

* from the 14th Century;
in the early 20th Century, 1 last = 12 dozen (144) hides.

Table 1.12 *Quantities of Furs, Pelts and Skins*   [14]

1 scordik	=	24 skins
1 binne	=	33 skins
1 timber	=	40 skins *
1 kipp †	=	30 lamb skins
	=	50 goat skins
1 hundred	=	5 score skins‡

note: calves skins were tanned by the dozen.

• for bear, ferret, fitch, martin, mink, otter, sable.

† and hence kipp being a large sack for storing fleece.

‡ for cat, coney, kid, lamb.

60 skins were used for one parchment roll (Table 1.7).

Table 1.13 Millions   [45]

British and European *	American
million = thousand x thousand (10^6)	million = thousand x thousand (10^6)
billion = million x million (10^{12})	billion = thousand x million (10^9)
trillion = million x billion (10^{18})	trillion = million x million (10^{12})
quadrillion = million x trillion (10^{24})	quadrillion = million x billion (10^{15})

* confirmed at the 9th General Conference on Weights and Measures (1948).

Note ~ 1 part per million (1 ppm) is equivalent to:

- 1 kilogram in 1000 tonnes
- 1 inch in 16 miles
- 6 square inch in 1 acre
- 1 minute in 690 days

Table 1.14 Ancient British Numerals   [34, 35]

1	= yana		11	=	yana-dik
2	= tana		12	=	tana-dik
3	= tethera		13	=	tethera-dik
4	= pethera		14	=	pethera-dik
5	= pimp		15	=	bumfit (pimpit)
6	= sethera		16	=	yana-bumfit
7	= lethera		17	=	tana-bumfit
8	= hovera		18	=	tethera-bumfit
9	= dovera		19	=	pethera-bumfit
10	= dik		20	=	gigit

Note: these numbers were used for counting sheep in Cumbria, Yorkshire and Lincolnshire, at least, into the 19th Century and were the cause of considerable correspondence in *The Athenaeum* in 1877 and in *Notes and Queries* in 1885.

Table 1.15 Multiples of the Power of Ten   [47]

Prefix	Symbol	Factor by which unit is multiplied
yotta	Y	10^{24}
zetta	Z	10^{21}
exa	E	10^{18}
peta	P	10^{15}
tera	T	10^{12}
giga	G	10^{9}
mega	M	10^{6}
quinta	q	10^{5}
myria		10^{4}
kilo	k	10^{3}
hecto	h	10^{2}
deca	da	10^{1}
deci	d	10^{-1}
centi	c	10^{-2}
milli	m	10^{-3}
micro	μ	10^{-6}
nano	n	10^{-9}
pico	p	10^{-12}
femto	f	10^{-15}
atto	a	10^{-18}
zepto	z	10^{-21}
yocto	y	10^{-24}

2. Length: Linear Measure

As mentioned in the Introduction, some linear measurements were derived from parts of the human body. The digit, inch, nail, palm, hand and span were based on finger and hand sizes, as shown in Fig 2.1; it should be noted that 1 span = 3 palms or ½ cubit. The nail is the distance from the second joint to the tip of the

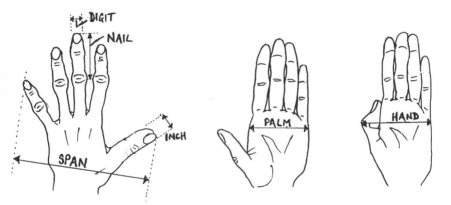

Fig 2.1 - Finger and hand sizes.

middle finger. The foot is related to finger sizes by being equal to 16 digits or 12 inches or 4 palms or 3 hands. Heroditus (484-424 BC) noted that the distance between the tips of the middle fingers on a man's outstretched arms was equal to six times the length of his foot. Marcus Vitruvius Pollio (1st Century BC) recognized this spread (a fades or fathom) to be four times a cubit, the distance from his elbow to his finger tips. Half of a fathom, a yard, was defined by Henry I (1100-35) as the distance from his nose to the tip of the middle finger on his outstretched arm. As a nail, being 2¼ inches, is a sixteenth of a yard it was later used to describe a sixteenth of other units. Leonardo da Vinci, with his passion for mathematics and anatomy, sketched his now famous Vitruvian man in 1490. An annotated version of Leonardo's work is shown in the frontispiece.

The stride or geometrical pace was accepted as the distance between the successive planting by a walking man of his right foot; a Roman, taking 1000 strides in conquered Britain would have walked a millarium - the Roman mile of

5000 feet. A step is half a stride or the distance between the planting of left and right feet by a walking man. If the man is imagined as a soldier on parade, it is understandable that a step is also termed a military pace. These relationships are shown in Table 2.1.

Linear measurements were also derived from agricultural practices (see Table 2.2), an inch being defined as 3 barleycorns taken from the centre of a mature head of barley and placed end to end; some authorities later identified that 1 barleycorn = 4 poppyseeds. Such measures, naturally, were not directly compatible with human body measurements. Whilst both body and agricultural measures were used from the 10th Century, attempts were made in the reign of Edward I, and confirmed by a decree of 1592, to reconcile these two systems of linear measurement, resulting in a series of units such as shown in Tables 2.3 to 2.5; and later, 12 hairs breadths were equated to 1 poppyseed. Furthermore, English shoe sizes are defined in one-third inch increments, size 8 being 11 inches, 9 being 11⅓, 10 being 11⅔ and 11 being 12 inches long for example; but whether these originated as barleycorn measurements is debatable. In 20th Century Britain the yard was still the legal unit of length, being the distance between two gold plugs on an iridium-platinum bar at 62°F held originally by the Board of Trade. In 1963, however, the yard was defined in terms of the metre.

Before the days of word-processors and computerized type-setting, typefounders used their own unique measurements (see Table 2.6) in the printing world to identify type sizes. Mercers used a wide variety of units to measure cloths of differing materials. In the 13th Century, an ell is equivalent to a yard, but it later becomes longer (see Table 2.7). A piece is a commonly used measure in the 15th and 16th Centuries, but this can vary from 10 yards for tartan to as much as 40 yards for buckram. The length and breadth of cloth also varies with the material: a length of straight cloth is 14 yards, its breadth 16 nails; a length of kersey (coarse woollen cloth originally from Suffolk) is 18 yards, its breadth 17 nails; a length of coloured cloth is 26 yards, its breadth 6 quarters; a length of ray cloth is 28 yards, its breadth 6 quarters; a length of worsted cloth is 29 to 31 yards, its breadth 7 quarters; a short worsted length is 14 to 15 yards. Even into the 20th Century, Dutch linens were imported into England being bought by the Flemish ell but sold by the English ell, while tapestry was sold in England by the Flemish ell. Some mercers' measures are shown in Tables 2.7 to 2.10. Needle sizes are given in Table 2.11. Units of length were employed in the construction of temples and monuments, as described in the Bible (see Table 2.12).

Table 2.1 Lengths Based on Body Measurements   [14, 40, 42]

1 digit	=	width of a man's middle finger
1 inch	=	width of a man's thumb at the root of the nail
1 nail	=	2¼ inches
1 palm	=	3 inches
1 hand	=	4 inches
1 shaftment	=	9 digits
	≈	6 inches (in fact 6.55 inches)
1 span *	=	9 inches
1 foot	=	16 digits
	=	12 inches
1 pes manualis	=	2 shaftments
	≈	1 foot (in fact 13.11 inches)
1 cubit	=	18 inches
1 yard	=	2 cubits
1 fathom	=	4 cubits
	=	6 feet
	=	2 yards
1 step †	=	2½ feet
1 stride ‡	=	2 steps
	=	5 feet
1 stade	=	125 strides
1 millarium	=	1000 strides

a hand is used to measure the height of a horse, a fathom to measure depths of mines and water (see Table 2.5).

* also termed a quarter, being a quarter of a yard.

† also termed a gradus or military pace.

‡ also termed a geometrical pace.

Table 2.2 Lengths Based on Agriculture   [14, 42]

1 inch	=	3 barleycorns *
1 rod, pole or perch †	=	2 manorial court measures ‡
1 furlong ¤	=	40 rods

* taken from the centre of a mature head of barley and placed end to end; and later equated to 4 poppyseeds or 48 hairs breadths.

† the width of a rood (Tables 2.3 & 3.4);   ‡ also termed a pall or paul (see Table 3.3).

¤ derived from a furrow-long - the length of a furrow that an ox-team would plough in a common field before stopping for a brief rest (see Table 3.1). Also called a flat, couture, quarentena and stadium.   It was later defined as one-eighth of a mile.

Table 2.3 Standardized Linear Measures   [15, 22, 40]

1 inch	=	12 lines *
	=	1000 mils
1 foot	=	12 inches
1 yard	=	3 feet
1 rod, pole or perch	=	16½ feet †
	=	5½ yards
1 furlong	=	40 rods
	=	220 yards
1 mile (English)	=	8 furlongs
	=	1760 yards
	=	5280 feet
1 mile (Scottish)	=	5920 feet
1 mile (Irish)	=	6720 feet
1 league	=	3 miles

* used in early 18th Century measurements and later for type (see Table 2.6); when used to measure the length of buttons, there were 40 lines to the inch.

† the perch, also termed a goad, gyrd, landyard or lugg, varied in length between common land and woodland into the 19th Century. An ell-ridge (= 60 luggs) was used in some districts.   But note, 1 manorial tenant measure = 6 ¾ feet (see Table 2.2).

Table 2.4 Land Surveyors' Measures   [42]

1 link	=	7.92 inches
1 pole	=	25 links
1 chain	=	100 links
	=	4 poles
	=	66 feet
1 furlong	=	10 chains
1 mile	=	80 chains

Note: a 7 yard diameter circle has a circumference of very nearly 1 chain (22 yards)

Table 2.5 Nautical Measures   [41, 42]

1 fathom	=	6 feet
1 chain	=	15 feet
1 log-line	=	450 feet
1 cable's length	=	100 fathoms (600 feet)
1 league	=	3 nautical miles
1 degree	=	60 nautical miles
	=	69.121 statute miles
1 International nautical mile *	=	10 cable's lengths
1 geographical mile †	=	2025.6 yards
1 British nautical mile	=	6080 feet
	=	2026.66 yards
	=	1.15 statute miles

* defined as one-sixtieth part of a degree of longitude at the equator; in actual fact 2023.23 yards, but in practice 2000 yards was used.   Now identified as 1852 metres.

† defined as one-sixtieth part of the mean degree of latitude.

Note: One knot = one British nautical mile per hour (but was used for many years incorrectly as a term for a British nautical mile).

Table 2.6 Typefounders' Measures   [22]

1 line	=	6 points *
1 em †	=	2 lines
1 inch	=	6 ems

* height of type.

† width of type, being equal to the height of the type used; derived from the letter m, originally having identical width and height. Also termed a pica.

Table 2.7 Cloth Measures   [14, 15, 40]

1 nail	=	2¼ inches
1 quarter	=	4 nails (9 inches)
1 yard	=	4 quarters (36 inches)
1 ell (English)	=	5 quarters (45 inches)
1 ell (French)	=	6 quarters (54 inches)
1 ell (Scottish) *	=	37 inches
1 ell (Flemish) †	=	3 quarters (27 inches)
1 plait	=	1⅛ yards
1 whole cloth	=	24 - 46 yards ‡
1 pack	=	10 whole cloths
1 fall (Scotland)	=	6 ells
1 chief (sindon)	=	12½ yards (10 ells)
1 chief (fustian)	=	17½ yards (14 ells)
1 piece (fustian)	=	30 yards (24 ells)
1 bolt	=	40 yards (32 ells)

* until 1803 when the English ell was adopted.

† also termed a stick or styke.   ‡ depending on the type of cloth and date.

Note: The Latin word ulna was used for both yard and ell even though these were different lengths!

Table 2.8 Cotton and Silk Measures   [6, 37, 42]

1 fold	=	36 inches
1 thread *	=	1½ yards
1 skein	=	80 threads (120 yards)
1 cut	=	70 yards
1 hank	=	7 skeins (840 yards)
	=	12 cuts
1 spindle	=	18 hanks (15,120 yards)

* also termed a pick.

Table 2.9 Worsted Measures   [6, 37, 42]

1 wrap* or lee	=	80 yards
1 hank	=	7 wraps (560 yards)
1 clue	=	4800 yards

* derived from the wrapping machine which makes 80 revolutions of 1 yard in circumference, giving 80 yards of worsted.

(A similar machine for cotton makes 80 revolutions of 1½ yards in circumference, giving 120 yards of cotton - see Table 2.8).

Table 2.10 Linen Measures   [42]

1 hank	=	300 yards
1 spindle	=	48 hanks (14,400 yards)
1 bundle	=	200 hanks

Table 2.11 Diameters of Needles   [6]

Descriptive Number	Diameter *
1	0.044 inch
2	0.040 inch
3	0.036 inch
4	0.032 inch
5	0.028 inch
6	0.024 inch
7	0.022 inch
8	0.020 inch
9	0.018 inch
10	0.016 inch

* measured half-way between the eye and the point.

Table 2.12 Biblical Lengths   [33]

finger	(Jeremiah Ch.42,v.21)	=	1 digit (Table 2.1)
handbreadth	(Exodus Ch.25,v.25)	=	1 hand
span	(Exodus Ch.28,v.16)	=	1 span
cubit	(Genesis Ch.6,v.15)	=	2 spans
fathom	(Acts Ch.27,v.28)	=	4 cubits
reed	(Ezekiel Ch.11,vv.3-5)	=	11 feet
line	(Ezekiel Ch.11,v.3)	=	80 cubits
furlong	(Luke Ch.24,v.13)	=	1 Greek furlong
mile	(Matthew Ch.5,v.41)	=	8 Greek furlongs
Sabbath Day's Journey	(Acts Ch.1,v.12)	=	1 mile *

* some authorities say 2 miles.

3. Area : Square Measure

Measurement of area was particularly relevant to arable land and used originally to determine its value or the amount needed to support a peasant family. One land unit was the hide, the area that a team of eight oxen could plough in an agricultural year, obviously dependent upon soil quality and terrain - fertility, topography and geology (see Tables 3.1 to 3.3); and because of the weather, an agricultural year was longer in the south of England than in the north. The more that land was ploughed and manured the greater its productivity became, and hence the absolute area of a hide decreased over the years. For example, the poor quality land around Battle in Sussex in the 11th Century was considered as having eight virgates to the hide but as the land was developed agriculturally it was reassessed at four virgates to the hide. Many other names for land areas are given in the tables below.

In early times most land was worked according to the feudal system and much of the population owned no land of their own; thus the varying sizes of hides, acres and associated areas mattered little to the average person. Howeve, when the manorial system permitted the transfer, sale and purchase of land from the 13th Century, its accurate surveying and measuring became a necessity and absolute sizes of land areas emerged, as shown in Tables 3.4 to 3.6.

Builders used their own terminology (Table 3.7) to describe areas of interest to their colleagues, while printers, publishers and paper suppliers developed a most colourful nomenclature for varying paper and book sizes. Attempts were made to standardize these throughout Europe (but not North America) in the mid-20th Century, with droll descriptions such as A5, B4 etc, as shown in Tables 3.8 to 3.11. For completion, circular measures are included in Table 3.12.

Table 3.1 Land Productivity Areas   [23, 40]

[all of these depend on the quality of soil and so have no absolute sizes]

1 hide	=	the area that a caruca (team of eight oxen) can plough in an agricultural year, sufficient to support a typical peasant family. Thus also termed a ploughland, ploughgate and husbandland. * Also termed a carucate and sulung † (Kent).
1 knight's fee	=	4 - 8 hides (usually 5 hides)
1 barony	=	40 hides
1 hide	=	8 oxgangs, oxlands, oxgates, bovates (East-Anglia), or nooks (Scotland and north of England).
	=	4 virgates ‡, yard-lands, yards of land, wista (Sussex), yokes or jugum (Kent).
	=	4 broad oxgangs.
1 broad oxgang	=	2 oxgangs (thus oxgang is sometimes termed a narrow oxgang).
1 oxgang	=	2 farthingdales, farthingholds, fardels or ferlings.
1 math	=	the area that a man can mow in a day (Hereford).
1 acre	=	the area that a team of eight oxen can plough in a morning, although often described as a day's work - the oxen were put out to pasture in the afternoons. Also termed an erws, quartentine and stang.

* in the north of England sometimes = ¼ hide.

† prior to the 9th Century a sulung = 2 hides.

‡ virgate was also (confusingly) used to describe ¼ acre.

When assessing land productivity the above relationships sometimes vary.

Table 3.2 Approximate Absolute Sizes of Productivity Areas [23]

1 oxgang	=	8 to 50 acres *
1 virgate	=	16 to 60 acres (normally 30 acres)
1 librate †	=	52 to 2000 acres (normally 52 acres)
1 hide	=	64 to 240 acres (normally 120 ‡ acres)
1 acre	=	4840 to 7840 sq yards (see Table 3.4)

* depending on the terrain and the quality of the soil.

† originally land worth £1 a year.

‡ the long hundred (see Table 1.1).

Table 3.3 Related Land Areas [23]

1 paulpiece	=	⅛ acre
1 hop acre *	≈	½ acre
1 tenantry acre	=	¾ acre
1 math †	≈	1 acre
1 woodacre ‡	=	1⅓ acres
1 markland	=	1 to 3 acres
1 acreland	=	8 to 20 acres
1 acreme	≈	10 acres
1 pottle	=	12 acres
1 verge	≈	15 to 30 acres
1 davoch ¤	≈	416 acres

* land supporting 1000 hop plants.

† see Table 3.1.

‡ derived from a woodland perch being larger than a common land perch.

¤ a variable Scottish unit.

Table 3.4 Accepted Land Sizes from 13ᵗʰ Century   [22]

1 acre	=	1 furlong (see Table 2.2) in length and 66 furrows of one foot wide in breadth *
	=	1 furlong in length and 4 rods or 4 poles or 4 perches in breadth *
	=	4840 square yards (most of England from Edward I)
	=	6760 square yards (Westmorland)
	=	6084 - 6104 square yards (Scotland)
	=	7840 square yards (Ireland)
1 rood	=	1 furlong in length and 1 rod in breadth

* This breadth of an acre became so useful that in the 17ᵗʰ Century Edmund Gunter gave it a specific unit, the chain (see Table 3.6).

Table 3.5 Generally-used English Square Measures   [15, 37,]

1 square foot	=	144 square inches
1 square yard	=	9 square feet
1 square rod, pole or perch	=	30¼ square yards
1 rood	=	40 square rods, poles or perches
1 acre	=	4 roods
	=	4840 square yards
1 square mile	=	640 acres

Table 3.6 Gunter's Square Land Measure   [40, 42]

1 square link	=	62.726 square inches
1 square pole	=	625 square links
1 square chain	=	16 square poles (10,000 square links)
1 acre	=	10 square chains
1 square mile	=	6400 square chains

Table 3.7 Square Building Measures   [42, 43]

1 square of flooring	=	100 square feet
1 rod of brickwork	=	272½ square feet
1 bay of slating	=	500 square feet
1 yard of land	=	30 acres
1 hide of land	=	1 hundred * acres

* the long or great hundred of 120.

Table 3.8 Sizes of Paper   [37, 42, 45]

[all sizes are in inches]

Name	Writing and Drawing Paper	Printing Paper	Brown (wrapping) Paper
Emperor	72x48		
Double Quad Crown		60x40	
Quad Imperial			58x45
Double Nicanee			56x45
Quad Royal			50x40
Antiquarian	53x31		
Casing			46x36
Saddleback			45x36
Quad Demy		45x35	
Double Imperial			45x29
Grand Eagle	42x28¾		
Quad Crown		40x30	
Double Elephant	40x26¾		
Double Royal		40x25	

[Table continued on next page]

Table 3.8 (contd) Sizes of Paper

[all sizes are in inches]

Name	Writing and Drawing Paper	Printing Paper	Brown (wrapping) Paper
Colombier	34½x23½		
Atlas	34x26		
Double Large Post	33x21	33x21	
Six Pound Grocers			32x22
Double Four Pound			31x21
Double Demy	31x20	35x22½	
Double Post	30½x19	31½x19½*	
Imperial	30x22	30x22	
Double Crown		30x20	
Imperial Cap			29x22
Elephant	28x23	28x23	34x24
Super Royal	27x19	27½x20½	
Double Foolscap	26½x16½	27x17	
Cartridge	26x21		
Haven Cap			26x21
Four Pound Grocers			26x20
Royal	24x19	25x20	
Sheet and half Foolscap	24½x13½		
Bag Cap			24x19½
Sheet and half Post		23½x19½	

[Table continued on next page]

Table 3.8 (contd) Sizes of Paper

[all sizes are in inches]

Name	Writing and Drawing Paper	Printing Paper	Brown (wrapping) Paper
Medium	22x17½	23x18†	
Sheet and third Foolscap	22x13½		
Kent Cap			21x18
Large Post	21x16½		
Copy or Draft	20x16		20x16½
Demy	20x15½	22½x17½	
Music Demy		20x15½	
Crown		20x15	
Post	19x15¼	19¼x15½‡	
Pinched Post	18½x14¾		
Foolscap	17x13½	17x13½	
Brief	16½x13¼		
Pott	15x12½		

* ref. 37 has 31¼x19¾

† ref. 37 has 24x19

‡ ref. 37 has 19½x15½

Table 3.9 International Paper Sizes [45]

Desig-nation	Size		Desig-nation	Size	
	mm	inches		mm	inches
A0	841x1198	33.11x46.81	B0	1000x1414	39.37x55.67
A1	594x841	23.39x33.11	B1	707x1000	27.83x39.37
A2	420x594	16.54x23.39	B2	500x707	19.68x27.83
A3	297x420	11.69x16.54	B3	353x500	13.90x19.68
A4	210x297	8.27x11.69	B4	250x353	9.84x13.90
A5	148x210	5.83x8.27	B5	176x250	6.93x9.84
A6	105x148	4.13x5.83	B6	125x176	4.92x6.93
A7	74x105	2.91x4.13	B7	88x125	3.46x4.92
A8	52x74	2.05x2.91	B8	62x88	2.44x3.46
A9	37x52	1.46x2.05	B9	44x62	1.73x2.44
A10	26x37	1.02x1.46	B10	31x44	1.22x1.73

Table 3.10 Paper Folding into Leaves & Pages

Name	Abbreviation	Paper Folded into leaves	Paper Folded into pages
Folio	Fo	2	4
Quarto	4to	4	8
Octavo	8vo	8	16
Duodecimo	12mo	12	24
Sextodecimo	16mo	16	32
Octodecimo	18mo	18	36
Vicesimo	20mo	20	40
Vicesimoquarto	24mo	24	48
Duoettricesimo	32mo	32	64

Table 3.11 Sizes of Bound Books   [45]

[all sizes are in inches]

Note: The height is followed by the width. Books with a width greater than their height are designed "ob"; eg ob medium Octavo (obM8) is 6 inches high x $9\frac{1}{2}$ inches wide.

Name	Size	Abbreviation
Imperial Folio	22x15	Impfol
Super Royal Folio	20x13$\frac{1}{2}$	suRfol
Royal Folio	20x12$\frac{1}{2}$	Rfol
Medium Folio	18x11$\frac{1}{2}$	Mfol
Demy Folio	17$\frac{1}{2}$x11$\frac{1}{4}$	Dfol
Crown Folio	15x10	Cfol
Post Folio	15$\frac{1}{4}$x9$\frac{1}{2}$	Postfol
Foolscap Folio	13$\frac{1}{2}$x8$\frac{1}{2}$	Ffol
Pott Folio	12$\frac{1}{2}$x7$\frac{3}{4}$	Pottfol
Imperial Quarto (4to)	15x11	Imp4
Super Royal 4to	13$\frac{1}{2}$x10	suR4
Royal 4to	12$\frac{1}{2}$x10	R4
Medium 4to	11$\frac{1}{2}$x9	M4
Demy 4to	11$\frac{1}{4}$x8$\frac{3}{4}$	D4
Crown 4to	10x7$\frac{1}{2}$	C4
Post 4to	9$\frac{1}{2}$x7$\frac{5}{8}$	Post4
Foolscap 4to	8$\frac{1}{2}$x6$\frac{3}{4}$	F4
Pott 4to	7$\frac{3}{4}$x6$\frac{1}{4}$	Pott4
Imperial Octavo(8vo)	11x7$\frac{1}{2}$	Imp8
Super Royal 8vo	10x6$\frac{3}{4}$	suR8

[Table continued on next page]

Table 3.11 (contd) Sizes of Bound Books

[all sizes are in inches]

Name	Size	Abbreviation
Royal 8vo	$10x6\frac{1}{4}$	R8
Medium 8vo	$9x5\frac{3}{4}$	M8
Demy 8vo	$8\frac{3}{4}x5\frac{5}{8}$	D8
Large Crown 8vo	$8x5\frac{1}{4}$	
Crown 8vo	$7\frac{1}{2}x5$	C8
Post 8vo	$7\frac{5}{8}x4\frac{7}{8}$	Post8
Foolscap 8vo	$6\frac{3}{4}x4\frac{1}{4}$	F8
Pott 8vo	$6\frac{1}{4}x3\frac{7}{8}$	Pott8
Demy 16mo	$5\frac{5}{8}x4\frac{3}{8}$	D16
Demy 18mo	$5\frac{3}{4}x3\frac{3}{4}$	D18
Music	$14x10\frac{1}{4}$	

Table 3.12 Circular Measures

[40]

1 minute	=	60 seconds
1 degree	=	60 minutes
1 sign	=	30 degrees
1 sextant	=	60 degrees
1 quadrant	=	90 degrees
1 grade	=	0.01 quadrant
1 circle	=	4 quadrants
	=	360 degrees
1 radian	=	57.3 degrees
1 circle	=	2π radians

4. Volume and Capacity: Cubic Measure

Goods being taken to market for sale, or even for exchange by barter, were carried in containers of somewhat similar shape and size; over the years these came to have reasonably consistent capacities. Bushels and pecks were the usual measures, particularly for dry goods such as grain and peas, salt and flour, even fish and coal, while less familiar measures (see Table 4.5) were also employed. Barrels and hogsheads, with pints and gallons, were used as measures of dry capacity as well as indicating volumes of fluids - although the absolute size of a barrel depended very much on the nature of its contents (see Tables 4.7 and 4.8). The barrel was also used as a variable measure of weight, which is described in Chapter 5. The gallon had a similar variant career being defined in 1290 by its capacity for 8 pounds (see Chapter 5) of wheat; a gallon was stated in 1706 to be 231 cubic inches and to today this remains the gallon recognized in the United States of America. However, in 1824 Britain redefined its gallon as an Imperial Gallon having the capacity of 10 Avoirdupois pounds of water, a volume of 277.274 cubic inches and confirmed in 1878 for solids and fluids (see Table 4.5).

Ale, beer and porter are combined in Table 4.7; whilst all these are infusions of malt from barley by fermentation, ale originally contained no hops and small-beer had a higher specific gravity, ie, was less alcoholic. Small beer was sold in the 18th Century at 2d a pint and hence was termed tuppenny. Porter, formerly termed three-threads or entire, is a mixture of ale, beer and tuppenny. In the 17th Century good ale cost 4d a gallon while panyers, a weak form of small-beer, was 1d a gallon. Black-jack, bombard, gaspin and piggin were leather "bottles" of an accepted (but not standard) size used mostly to transport ale, although in country areas it was drunk directly from these vessels. Containers of varying sizes, solely for drinking, included the coaching glass and tumbler, both with round bases to encourage immediate consumption, the crinze, cup (prunet and mether-cup, for example), goblet, jorum, mazer, mug, pot, quaich, rummer, tappit-hen and whiskin.

In times when wood was the main building material and source of fuel, sizes of timber and firewood bundles were critical, resulting in specific names (see Table 4.4) being used to identify particular amounts. Care should be taken when relating Scottish measures of drink (see Tables 4.9 to 4.11) to English quantities because of the difference in quart sizes across the Border; at one stage 1 Scottish quart equalled 3 English quarts. Apothecaries and pharmaceutical chemists developed their own fluid capacity measures (Tables 4.12 and 4.13), the scruple giving us the word scrupulous to describe their honesty and precision. Some Biblical capacities are provided in Tables 4.14 and 4.15.

Table 4.1 Basic Volume Measures   [38, 42]

1 cubic foot	=	1728 cubic inches
1 cubic yard	=	27 cubic feet
1 cartload	=	30 * cubic feet

* sometimes 27 cubic feet, ie, one cubic yard.

1 cubic foot of water = 62.4 gallons and weighs 1000 Avoirdupois ounces (see Tables 4.5 and 5.5 and footnotes).

Table 4.2 Timber Measures   [37, 42, 43]

A plank	=	10* inches wide and 2* inches thick
A deal	=	9 inches wide and 3† inches thick
A board	=	9 inches wide and 1½‡ inches thick
A floor-board	=	6 to 7 inches wide and 1 to 1¼ inches thick
1 ton (cargo) or load	=	40 ▫ cubic feet unhewn timber
	=	50 cubic feet squared timber
	=	600 square feet of 1 inch board
1 stack	=	108 cubic feet
1 cord	=	128 ⌧ cubic feet
1 standard (Christiania)	=	103⅛ cubic feet
1 standard (Leningrad)	=	165 cubic feet
1 standard (London)	=	270 cubic feet
1 hundred	=	120 deals
1 square	=	100 superficial feet of planking

* or more.   † sometimes 2 inches thick.   ‡ or less.

▫ sometimes 42 cubic feet.   ⌧ sometimes 120 cubic feet.

The Dublin Standard was identical to the London Standard.

Table 4.3 Builders' Measures   [22, 40]

A stock * brick	=	$8\frac{3}{4}$ x $4\frac{1}{4}$ x $2\frac{3}{4}$
A Welsh † fire-brick	=	9 x $4\frac{1}{2}$ x $2\frac{3}{4}$
A paving brick	=	9 x $4\frac{1}{2}$ x $1\frac{3}{4}$
A Dutch clinker brick	=	$9\frac{1}{4}$ x 3 x $1\frac{1}{2}$
A square tile	=	$9\frac{3}{4}$ x $9\frac{3}{4}$ x 1
(also)	=	6 x 6 x 1

Note: brick and tile sizes in inches.

* also termed a kiln brick.

† also termed a Welch fire-brick. Prior to the 19th Century bricks were often 9 x $4\frac{1}{2}$ x $2\frac{1}{4}$ inches, ie, a span x a half-span x a nail.

A rod of brickwork $16\frac{1}{2}$ feet x $16\frac{1}{2}$ feet and one-and-a-half bricks thick is 306 cubic feet or $11\frac{1}{3}$ cubic yards.

As a linear rod is approximately 5 metres, a rod of brickwork (25 square metres) one-and-a-half bricks thick is approximately 10 cubic metres.

Table 4.4 Firewood Measures   [14]

Measure	Length	Circumference
1 faggot	36 inches	24 inches
1 billet	40 inches	$7\frac{1}{2}$ inches
1 cast	40 inches	10 inches
cast of 2	40 inches	14 inches
No.1 shid *	48 inches	16 inches
No.2 shid	48 inches	23 inches
No.3 shid	48 inches	28 inches
No.4 shid	48 inches	33 inches
No.5 shid	48 inches	38 inches

Note: not in common use after the early 17th Century.
* also termed a shide and taleshid.

Table 4.5 Dry Capacities [14, 15, 37, 40, 42]

1 pint	=	4 gills
1 quart	=	2 pints
1 pottle *	=	2 quarts (4 pints)
1 gallon †	=	2 pottles (8 pints)
1 peck ‡	=	2 gallons
	=	4 beatments
1 tovet (tuffet)	=	2 pecks
1 bushel	=	4 pecks (8 gallons)
1 bucket (of chalk)	=	1½ bushels
1 strike or raser	=	2 bushels
1 bag	=	3 bushels
1 coombe (of grain)	=	4 bushels
1 seam	=	2 coombes
1 sack (of coal)	=	4 bushels
1 sack (of flour)	=	5 bushels
	=	1 porter's load
1 quarter ¤	=	8 bushels
1 chaldron	=	12 bags (36 bushels)
1 wey ⧖	=	5 quarters (40 bushels)
1 last	=	2 weys

[table continued on next page]

* termed a forpit or lippie in Scotland.

† also termed a lagen.

‡ termed a kishon on the Isle of Man.

¤ also termed a seam, hence a coombe was termed a half-quarter.

⧖ also termed a load or horse-load. For salt 1 wey = 42 bushels, 1 last = 10 weys (420 bushels).

From 1730 1 sack of coal or coke = 3 bushels.
1 chaldron of coal = 36 bushels from 1664; in the 16th Century it had been 32.bushels.

Table 4.5 (contd) Dry Capacities

1 standard gallon §	=	277.274 cubic inches
1 standard bushel	=	2218.19 cubic inches
1 Winchester corn bushel	=	2150.4 cubic inches
	≈	7¾ gallons

§ this is the value stated in the 1824 Statute; however, when its volume was measured accurately in 1931-2 it was found to be 277.421 cubic inches.

Since 1878 a standard (Imperial) gallon has been defined as the capacity of 10 Avoirdupois pounds of distilled water at 62°F under 30 inches barometric pressure.

The Winchester corn bushel was defined in 1696.

The coal bushel was defined in 1713 but when its volume was measured in 1872 it was found to be 2222 cubic inches.

Table 4.6 Fish Measures   [37, 42]

1 cran of herrings	=	37½ gallons
1 barrel of cured herrings (Scotland)	=	26⅔ gallons *
1 firkin of salmon	=	10½ gallons
1 kilderkin of salmon	=	21 gallons
1 barrel of salmon	=	35 - 42 gallons
1 butt of salmon	=	84 gallons
1 last of salmon	=	6 butts
	=	504 gallons

* this can be up to 30 gallons for herrings and anchovies.

Table 4.7 Ale, Beer and Porter Capacities   [14, 15, 37, 42]

1 pint	=	4 gills
	=	5 ponies
1 quart	=	2 pints
1 gallon	=	4 quarts [quarter gallons]
1 pin *	=	4½ gallons
1 firkin *	=	9 gallons
	=	2 pins
1 kilderkin *	=	2 firkins (18 gallons)
1 barrel *	=	2 kilderkins (36 gallons)
1 hogshead *	=	3 kilderkins (54 gallons)
1 puncheon *	=	2 barrels (72 gallons)
1 butt *	=	2 hogsheads (108 gallons)
1 American barrel	=	30 gallons
1 gallon	=	6 bottles
1 leager	=	164 gallons

1 jug of ale contains 1 pint.

1 tankard of ale contains 1 quart.

1 flagon or pitcher contains 1 gallon.

1 long glass or yard of ale contains 2¾ to 3½ pints.

* standard sizes of brewers' casks into the mid-20th Century.

Notes: A barrel of ale originally contained 32 gallons as an ale firkin equalled 8 gallons; in 1688 an ale barrel was changed to 34 gallons but in 1803 was standardized at 36 gallons, as shown above.

A barrel of beer originally contained 36 gallons; in 1688 a beer barrel was changed to 34 gallons and reverted to 36 gallons in 1803.

The yard of ale originated as a practical joke requiring the drinker to consume the contents at once - the glass is about a yard long and if tilted sharply empties its contents over the drinker.

Table 4.8 Wine, Spirits, Cider and Vinegar Capacities (also used for Oil and Honey) [14, 22, 37, 41, 42]

1 pint	=	4 gills *
1 quart	=	2 pints
1 gallon	=	4 quarts
1 sextary (sester)	=	4 gallons
1 anker	=	10 gallons
1 runlet (rundel)	=	18 gallons
1 barrel	=	31½ gallons
1 tierce †	=	42 gallons
1 hogshead	=	2 barrels (63 gallons)
1 puncheon ‡	=	2 tierces (84 gallons)
1 pipe ¤	=	2 hogsheads (126 gallons)
1 pipe	=	3 tierces
1 tun (tonnel)	=	2 pipes (252 gallons)
	=	3 puncheons
1 rode	=	2 tuns (≈ 500 gallons)

Note: the above measures are based on a wine gallon of 231 cubic inches; in the 16th Century, at least, the storage volumes of the barrel, hogshead, pipe, tun, and rode held a greater number of gallons than the retail volumes (eg, 1 tun storage = 250 gallons, 1 tun retail = 240 gallons); the tun is sometimes termed a vat. The Spanish wine measure arroba (approximately 3 gallons) was sometimes used by the British.

* a gill is also termed a quartern; in the north of England one gill = ½ pint, in which case the ¼ pint is termed a noggin or jack. Colloquially an eighth pint is termed a jock or dram and a sixteenth pint a joey.

1 gallon wine weighs approximately 8 pounds Avoirdupois.

8 gallons wine occupy the same volume as 1 bushel wheat (see Table 4.5).

† also termed an almer, aum or awm, although the latter two terms were mostly applied to wine imported from Holland; hence 1 aume ≈ 4 anker.

‡ also termed a tertian.

¤ also termed a butt.

Table 4.9 Scottish Liquid Capacities [37]

1 mutchkin	=	4 gills
1 choppin	=	2 mutchkins
1 pint	=	2 choppins
1 puncheon of Scotch Whisky	=	112 to 120 gallons

Note: ref. 37 has 1 pint = 8 choppins, but = 2 choppins from the 1932 edition.

A whisky bottle in Scotland was known as a "whisky quart" or "reputed quart" but was ⅔ Imperial quart and a similar size to an English wine or spirits bottle, see note to Table 4.10.

Table 4.10 Champagne and Bordeaux Bottle Capacities

1 Bottle *	=	0.75 litre		
1 Magnum	=	2 bottles	=	1.5 litres
1 Jeroboam	=	4 bottles	=	3 litres
1 Rehoboam †	=	6 bottles	=	4.5 litres
1 Methuselam	=	8 bottles	=	6 litres
1 Salmanazar	=	12 bottles	=	9 litres
1 Balthazar	=	16 bottles	=	12 litres
1 Nebuchadnezzar	=	20 bottles	=	15 litres

* In England a bottle of wine or spirits was traditionally one-sixth of a gallon, ie, 26⅔ fluid ounces (46.24 cubic inches), approximately 1½ pints. By the 1990s bottles of wine were available containing only 0.7 litre.

Unofficially, a quarter-of-a-bottle was known as a nip, and an eighth-of-a-bottle as a baby.

† Approximately 1 gallon.

Table 4.11 Miscellaneous Liquid Capacities [37]

1 pipe of Madeira	=	92 gallons
1 pipe of Teneriffe	=	100 gallons
1 pipe of Cider	=	100 - 118 gallons
1 pipe of Malaga	=	105 gallons
1 pipe of Sherry	=	108 gallons
1 pipe of Port	=	115 gallons
1 pipe of Lisbon	=	117 gallons
1 hogshead (aum) of Hock, Rhine and Moselle	=	30 gallons
1 hogshead of Claret	=	46 gallons
1 hogshead of Tent	=	54 gallons
1 hogshead of Rum	=	54 - 60 gallons
1 hogshead of Brandy	=	57 gallons
1 hogshead of Cape	=	92 gallons
1 hogshead of Marsala Bronte	=	93 gallons
1 puncheon of Rum	=	90 - 100 gallons
1 puncheon of Brandy	=	100 - 110 gallons
1 puncheon of Scotch Whisky	=	112 - 120 gallons
Quarter-cask of Brandy	=	28 gallons

Notes: The above were almost the only wine imports into the British Isles until the mid-20th Century; Madeira and Teneriffe being fortified whites from the Madeira and Canary islands; Malaga being a fortified red or white from Malaga, Southern Spain; Port and Lisbon being fortified, and originally exclusively red, from Portugal; Hock, Rhine and Moselle being white wines from Hochheim, and the valleys of the Rhine and Moselle rivers, Germany; Claret being a red from Burgundy, France, Tent being a sweet red from Spain; Cape being a white from the Cape of Good Hope, South Africa; Marsala Bronte being a sweet fortified wine from Sicily.

Table 4.12 Apothecaries' Fluid Capacities   [37, 41, 42]

1 fluid scruple	=	20 minims
1 fluid drachm	=	3 fluid scruples
1 fluid ounce	=	8 fluid drachms
1 pint *	=	20 fluid ounces
1 corbyn	=	40 fluid ounces (2 pints)
1 Winchester quart	=	80 fluid ounces (4 pints)
1 gallon †	=	160 fluid ounces (8 pints)

* also termed octarius (O).

† also termed congius (C or Cong).

see also Table 5.4.

Table 4.13 Approximate Medicine Capacities   [40, 42]

1 teaspoonful	=	1 fluid drachm
	=	60 drops
1 dessertspoonful	=	2 fluid drachms
1 tablespoonful	=	4 fluid drachms
1 wineglassful	=	2 fluid ounces
1 teacupful	=	3 fluid ounces

Note: the above are obviously only approximate as wineglasses and teacups vary in size. The 1618 London Pharmacopoeia gives the tablespoon as 3 fluid drachms and the wineglassful as $1\frac{1}{2}$ fluid ounces.

Table 4.14 Biblical Dry Capacities [33]

1 pot	(Mark Ch.7,v.4)	=	1½ pints
1 cab	(II Kings Ch.6,v.25)	=	2 pints
1 chenix	(Revelation Ch.6,v.6)	=	2 pints
1 omer	(Exodus Ch.16,v.36)	≈	3 pints
1 tenth-deal	(Exodus Ch.29,v.4)	≈	3 pints
1 seah	(Matthew Ch.13,v.33)	≈	2 gallons
1 bath or ephah	(Ezekiel Ch.45,v.11)	≈	6 gallons
1 homer	(Numbers Ch.11,v.32 (Hosea Ch.3,v.2)	≈	16 gallons

Table 4.15 Biblical Fluid Capacities [33]

1 log *	(Leviticus Ch.16,v.10)	=	¾ pint
1 hin	(Exodus Ch.29,v.4)	=	10 pints
1 bath	(I Kings Ch.7,v.26)	=	60 pints
		=	6 hins
1 firkin	(John Ch.2,v.6)	=	9 gallons
1 cor or homer	(Ezekiel Ch.45,v.14)	=	75 gallons
	(Isaiah Ch.5,v.10)	=	10 baths

* equal to six egg-shells full

[27]

Jedediah Buxton of Elmton, Chesterfield, Derbyshire proved in 1751 that:

200 barleycorns, 300 wheatcorns, 512 ryecorns, 180 oats, 40 peas, 25 beans, 80 vetches, 100 lentils, and 2304 one inch long hairs can be contained in one solid inch.

5. Weight and Mass

Years ago goods, particularly at markets, were weighed on balances or scales having a centrally supported beam with a pan suspended from each end. The items were placed on one pan and weights, normally iron or brass, added to the other pan until the beam was horizontal (although see the note to Table 5.15). The sum of the weights added to the pan was the actual weight in pounds or ounces, or even barleycorns etc, of the goods. Auncels were scales which either used false weights or could be manipulated by the weigher to tip the balance in his favour. Because of this fraud, auncels were banned from 1428 [identified by Wilkins in *Concilia iii, 516*] , although they were still being used in the 17th Century. A steelyard was another type of balance which, by having its fulcrum off-centre, enabled heavy goods to be weighed with relatively small weights: for example, a 7 pound weight at 24 inches from the fulcrum counter-balances a 28 pound item at 6 inches from the fulcrum.

In many cases we should be identifying mass, not weight. Strictly, the weight of an item depends on the force exerted on it by gravity, while mass is the amount of matter in that item. If, for example, the absolute weight of an item is measured by a spring-balance at the bottom of a mine and then on the top of a mountain, it will weigh less at the top of the mountain as it has a lower gravitational attraction there, even though its mass has not altered. On the moon, where the gravitational force is a sixth of that on earth, the item will weigh six times lighter and a spring-balance will indicate this. In practice not many of us or our ancestors travelled to the moon; even so, for goods being weighed in a particular market on a beam balance or steelyard the difference between mass and weight is of no consequence as two items with equal masses have equal weights under identical conditions. Accordingly, the veracity of any iron and brass weights is important and so national and local standards, which were the subject of a number of Acts of Parliament, were used to check the weights used by tradesmen.

Prior to the 20th Century there were several different series of pound and ounce weights, derived from the different ancient purposes for which they had been used. The Troy, Merchantile, Tower, Apothecaries', Avoirdupois and Postal systems are shown in Tables 5.1 to 5.7. Apart from the Roman pound or libra of 5050 grains, which is not considered here, the Troy pound is one of the oldest weights in England, although named after the French business city of Troyes; the Troy pound equated to the monetary pound sterling which contained 240 pennies (see Chapter 6). Originally a penny contained a pennyworth of almost pure silver which had the same weight as 24 grains of barleycorn. Thus a Troy pennyweight was defined as 24 Troy grains, and a Troy pound of 240 pennies weighed 24x240 = 5760 Troy grains. The Troy pound was divided into 12 Troy ounces, thus each Troy ounce had the same weight as 480 Troy grains, ie, 480÷24 = 20 Troy pennyweights. An Act in 1853 declared the Troy ounce to be the standard for the sale of bullion and, although the Troy pound was abolished in 1878, Troy ounces remained, albeit redefined, even in the 1985 Weights and Measures Act.

The Tower or Saxon pound used by the Royal Mint (housed in the Tower of London, and hence the pound's name), was equated to the monetary pound of 240 pennies but assumed that a silver penny equalled 22½ barleycorns. Thus a Tower pound, which was never a trade pound, solely a weight of audit, weighed 22½x240 = 5400 Tower grains. The Tower pound was also divided into 12 Tower ounces, so that one Tower ounce equalled 450 Tower grains, ie, 450÷22½ = 20 Tower pennyweights. Tower weight was abolished in 1527 in favour of the Troy system.

The Merchantile or Commercial pound (libra mercatoria) was based on 16 Tower ounces and thus weighed 16x450 = 7200 Tower barleycorn grains. Comparing this with a Troy ounce weighing 480 barleycorns, the Merchantile pound contained 7200÷480 = 15 Troy ounces. Thus a Merchantile pound = 300 Troy pennyweights or 320 Tower pennyweights. Now, 300 pennies in monetary terms is 25 shillings (see Chapter 6), thus the Merchantile pound was sometimes termed a pound of 25 shillingsweight Troy. Equally, as in monetary terms a mark is 13/4, ie, 160 pennies, the Merchantile pound (320 Tower pennyweights) was termed a Tower doublemark. Furthermore, as the Merchantile pound comprised 16 Tower ounces, the mark was equated to 8 ounces.

The Apothecaries' pound and ounce were identical to the Troy pound and ounce in being equal in weight respectively to 5760 and 480 grains of barleycorn. The Apothecaries' system differed from the Troy system in not referring to pennyweights and was subdivided into drachms and scruples. It was abolished in England on 1 January 1971.

The Avoirdupois pound, which came into common usage in the early 15th Century, was based on 16 ounces and equated to 7000 grains, such that the Avoirdupois ounce was 437½ grains; whilst this is obviously less than the Troy ounce, many commentators and Parliament as well, were confused about this discrepancy for over 200 years until 1588. The similarity with several European pounds with 16 sub-units and the ease of dividing 16 ounces, compared with 15 of the Merchantile pound, led to the popularity of the Avoirdupois pound, particularly in the weighing of wool. The importance of the wool trade caused the Avoirdupois system to eventually become the national standard.

The Postal pound was not a separate weight; however, after the debut of the Penny Post in 1840, the English Post Office developed a system of letter delivery charges based on weights in increments of half-ounces Avoirdupois, each termed one Postage (see Table 5.6). One-third and two-thirds ounce weights were also used after 1869, following an arrangement with the French postal authorities.

Similarly to certain containers becoming identified as holding specific capacities of popular goods, as described in Chapter 4, some containers became accepted as holding consistent masses or weights of particular items. Although these were not standardized measures, they were generally acknowledged as being consistent enough to be acceptable. For example, a sack of coal or a bag of cocoa always weighed a hundredweight of 112 Avoirdupois pounds, a carton of plums consistently weighed 9 pounds while a cask of nutmegs weighed 200 pounds. Pockets, tubs, chests, cartons, barrels, baskets and drums are other containers recognized as holding regular weights of specific commodities, many of which are shown in the following tables. The Exchequer became interested in accurate weights of wool when imposing a wool tax to raise revenue (see Chapmans Records Cameo, *Pre-1841 Censuses and Population Listings in the British Isles*). Wool was weighed on trones (scales) by a tronager using 7 and 14 pound lead or bronze weights, and taxed in 1467 at a penny per tod.

Table 5.1 Troy Weights   [15, 38, 44]

1 Troy pennyweight (dwt)	=	24 Troy grains * (gr)
1 Troy ounce (oz)	=	20 pennyweight (dwt)
1 Troy pound (lb) †	=	12 Troy ounces (oz) †
1 Troy hundredweight (cwt)	=	100 Troy pounds
1 Troy ounce	=	480 Troy grains
1 Troy pound	=	5760 Troy grains

* of barleycorn.   † from the Latin/Italian libra and onza.

Table 5.2 Merchantile Weights   [3]

1 Merchantile pound *	=	15 Troy ounces
	=	300 Troy pennyweights
	=	7200 Troy grains
1 fotmal †	=	70 Merchantile pounds
1 sack	=	5 fotmals

* also termed a Commercial pound (libra mercatoria).
† also termed a fotmel and formell

Table 5.3 Tower Weights   [3]

1 Tower pound	=	weight of 240 silver pennies
1 Tower ounce	=	weight of 20 silver pennies
1 Tower pound	=	5400 Troy grains
1 Tower ounce	=	450 Troy grains
1 silver penny	=	22½ Troy grains

Table 5.4 Apothecaries' Weights   [15, 42]

1 Apothecaries' scruple (Э)	=	20 Apothecaries' grains
1 Apothecaries' drachm (Ʒ)	=	3 Apothecaries' scruples
1 Apothecaries' ounce (℥)	=	8 Apothecaries' drachms
1 Apothecaries' pound (lb)	=	12 Apothecaries' ounces
1 Apothecaries' drachm	=	60 Apothecaries' grains *
1 Apothecaries' ounce	=	480 Apothecaries' grains
1 Apothecaries' pound	=	5760 Apothecaries' grains

* of barleycorns
see also Table 4.12.

Table 5.5 *Avoirdupois Weights* [15, 43]

1 ounce (oz)	=	16 drams
1 pound (lb)	=	16 ounces
1 stone	=	14 pounds
1 quarter (qr)	· =	2 stones
	=	28 Avoirdupois pounds
1 fotmal	=	72 Avoirdupois pounds
1 hundredweight (cwt)	=	4 quarters
	=	112 Avoirdupois pounds
1 ton *	=	20 hundredweights
	=	2240 Avoirdupois pounds
1 short ton	=	2000 Avoirdupois pounds
1 cental †	=	100 Avoirdupois pounds
1 kip ‡	=	1000 Avoirdupois pounds
1 Avoirdupois pound	=	7000 Troy grains

* also termed a long ton.
† abolished in 1978; also termed a short hundredweight.
‡ strictly a unit of force.
1 cubic foot of water at 62°F and 30 inches pressure weighs 1000 Avoirdupois ounces (see also Table 4.5).

Table 5.6 *Postal Weights*

1 Postage (P)	=	½ Avoirdupois ounce
2 Postages (P/2)	–	1 Avoirdupois ounce
4 Postages (P/4)	=	2 Avoirdupois ounces

Table 5.7 Relationships between various Pounds and Ounces

1 Troy pound	=	0.823 Avoirdupois pound
1 Tower pound	=	0.771 Avoirdupois pound
1 Merchantile pound	=	1.029 Avoirdupois pounds
1 Apothecaries' pound	=	0.823 Avoirdupois pound
1 Troy ounce	=	1.097 Avoirdupois ounces
1 Tower ounce	=	1.029 Avoirdupois ounces
1 Apothecaries' ounce	=	1.097 Avoirdupois ounces

Table 5.8 Grain Varieties' Weights

1 bushel barley	=	56 * pounds
1 bushel maize	=	60 pounds
1 bushel oats	=	39 pounds
1 bushel rye	=	60 pounds
1 bushel wheat	=	60 † pounds
1 bushel foreign wheat	=	62 pounds
1 jar wheat	=	52 pounds
1 quarter wheat	=	480 pounds (8 bushels)

* variable, often 50 pounds.

† variable, often 56 pounds.

Table 5.9 Hops Weights [40]

1 pocket	=	1½ to 2 hundredweights
1 bag	=	280 pounds

Table 5.10 Bread and Flour Weights [37, 42]

1 quartern of flour	=	3 pounds, 8 ounces Avoirdupois
1 quartern of bread	=	4 pounds, 5 ounces, 8½ drams Avoirdupois
1 peck of flour	=	14 pounds Avoirdupois
1 peck of bread	=	17 pounds, 6 ounces, 2 drams Avoirdupois
1 bushel of flour	=	56 pounds (4 pecks)
1 boll of flour	=	140 pounds (10 pecks)
1 barrel of flour	=	196 pounds
1 sack of flour	=	280 pounds (5 bushels) (2 bolls)

Note: from the 18th Century, the extra ounces and drams of bread weights were slowly disregarded and bread was sold in loaves weighing 4 pounds and 2 Avoirdupois pounds, usually termed quartern and half-quartern loaves; notwithstanding, bakers were not legally permitted to sell bread by the quartern or peck - but see Table 6.5.

Table 5.11 Hay and Straw Weights [37, 40, 42]

1 bundle straw	=	24 pounds
1 bolting straw	=	28 pounds
1 truss straw	=	36 pounds
1 truss old hay	=	56 pounds
1 truss new hay	=	60 pounds
1 square yard new hay	=	6 stones
1 square yard oldish hay	=	8 stones
1 square yard old hay	=	9 stones
1 load	=	36 trusses
1 load straw	=	11 cwt, 2qrs, 8lbs
1 load * old hay	=	18 cwt
1 load * new hay	=	19 cwt, 1 qr, 4lbs

* referred to as a ton of hay; a small load is a jagg.

Hay is regarded as old after 29 September.

Table 5.12 Meat Weights   [40, 42]

1 stone	=	8 pounds *
1 barrel	=	25 stone (beef)
	=	28 stone (pork)
1 piece (Irish beef)	=	8 pounds
1 tierce (Irish beef)	=	38 pieces
1 piece (Irish pork)	=	4 pounds
1 tierce (Irish pork)	=	80 pieces

* until 1939.

Note: the former practice of selling meat by the hand, the amount that a butcher could hold in one hand and judge as a suitable weight was not encouraged; although weighed hands of pork were still sold in some parts of England at the end of the 20th Century.

Table 5.13 Butter and Cheese Weights   [14, 42]

1 clove	=	8 pounds *
1 stone	=	2 cloves
1 wey (Suffolk)	=	16 stone
1 wey (Essex)	=	21 stone
1 firkin (butter)	=	56 pounds †
1 tub	=	1½ firkins
1 barrel	=	4 firkins

* in the 16th Century, although the cheese clove = 8 pounds, 1 clove of butter = 7 Avoirdupois pounds; hence a Suffolk wey of butter (32 cloves) = 224 pounds.

† this amount was also termed a keg or box. A half-box of lard was termed a pail. In the 16th Century 1 firkin of butter = 57½ Avoirdupois pounds, a kilderkin = 115 pounds and 1 barrel = 230 Avoirdupois pounds (256 pounds with cask), ie, the cask was supposed to weigh 26 Avoirdupois pounds; but a commentator noted that some casks weighed 32 pounds so that purchasers received only 224 pounds of butter - the amount shown in Table 5.13 above, which still applied in the 20th Century.

Table 5.14 Soap Weights   [37, 40]

1 firkin	=	64 pounds *
1 barrel	=	256 pounds *
1 chest	=	3¼ hundredweights

* in the 16th Century 1 firkin soap = 62 pounds, 1 kilderkin = 124 pounds,
   1 barrel = 248 pounds Avoirdupois (280 pounds with the cask).

Table 5.15 Wool Weights   [14, 37, 42]

1 clove *	=	7 pounds
1 stone	=	2 cloves (14 pounds)
1 tod †	=	2 stones (28 pounds)
1 wey	=	6½ tods (182 pounds)
1 pack	=	240 pounds
1 sack	=	2 weys (13 tods = 364 pounds)
1 sarpler ‡	=	2 sacks
	=	30 carks
1 last	=	12 sacks ¤
1 score	=	20 pounds
1 pack	=	12 score

* also termed a nail, being a sixteenth of a hundredweight.

† identical to one Avoirdupois quarter.

‡ also termed a pocket; a poke is a larger, variable, measure.

¤ equal to 39 hundredweights.

Note: during the 13th Century wool was weighed by the sack on an inclined beam which gave a value of 350 pounds; by the 14th Century the horizontal beam was customary which required a sack of wool to be balanced by 364 pounds, a value it retained for 600 years.

Table 5.16 Glass Weights   [42]

1 stone	=	5 pounds
1 seam	=	24 stone

Table 5.17 Coal and Coke Weights   [37, 42]

1 stone	=	14 pounds
1 quarter	=	2 stone
1 half-hundredweight	=	4 stone
1 hundredweight	=	112 pounds
1 sack (coal)	=	1 hundredweight
1 double sack	=	2 hundredweights
12 sacks	=	1 chaldon
1 keel *	=	21 tons, 4 hundredweights
1 shipload	=	424 tons
1 room	=	7 tons
1 chaldron	=	25½ hundredweights +

* also called a barge.   + the Newcastle chaldron varied considerably.
For capacities of sacks see Table 4.5.

Table 5.18 Gunpowder Weights   [14, 37]

1 barrel	=	100 pounds
1 last	=	24 barrels

Table 5.19 Iron Weights   [14]

1 sheaf	=	30 gads
1 burden	=	6 * sheaves

* occasionally 12. See Table 5.37 for steel.

Table 5.20 Lead and Tin Weights [14]

1 fotmal *	=	72 pounds Avoirdupois
1 sack	=	5 fotmals
	=	360 pounds Avoirdupois
1 load	=	6 sacks
	=	2160 pounds Avoirdupois
1 bing (ore)	=	8 hundredweights
1 fodder †	=	6 x 364 pounds Avoirdupois
	=	6 x 26 stones
	=	19½ hundredweights

* also termed a fotmel or formell; a 16th Century writer commented that 1 formell of lead = 70 pounds and 1 load, charge or fodder = 30 formells (2100 pounds), he further stated that 1 hundredweight at London = 112 pounds Avoirdupois, whereas 1 hundredweight at the King's Beam in Cornwall = 120 pounds Avoirdupois.

† also termed a fother.

Table 5.21 Pearl, Diamond and Bullion Weights [14, 37, 42]

1 English carat *	=	4 pearl or diamond grains
	=	3.17 Troy grains
1 Troy ounce	=	151.5 English carats
Pure gold	=	24 carats fine
18 carat gold	=	eighteen-twentyfourth's pure gold
9 carat gold	=	nine-twentyfourth's pure gold
1 bar gold	=	400 Troy ounces †
1 bar silver	=	1000 to 1100 Troy ounces
1 metric carat ‡	=	⅕ gram (200 mg)

* derived from the carob plant seed.

† 27 Avoirdupois pounds.

‡ precious stones had to be weighed by the metric carat from 1920 or by Troy ounces (480 grains) divided decimally.

Table 5.22 Sugar Weights   [37, 40]

from East Indies and Mauritius:		
1 bag *	=	112 to 196 pounds
	=	1 to 1¾ hundredweights
from West Indies:		
1 tierce	=	7 to 9 hundredweights
1 hogshead	=	13 to 16 hundredweights

* also termed a matt in Mauritius.

Table 5.23 Tea Weights   [37, 40]

1 caddy *	=	1⅓ pounds
1 chest (Hyson † tea)	=	60 to 80 pounds
1 chest (Congou ‡ tea)	=	80 pounds
1 chest (Ceylon) tea	=	120 pounds
1 chest (Indian tea)	=	126 pounds

* and hence the household container for tea; also termed a catty, from the Javanese, kati, meaning measure.

† green China tea, but contains up to 100 pounds by 1935.

‡ black China tea, but contains up to 100 pounds by 1935.

Table 5.24 Coffee Weights   [37, 40]

1 barrel *	=	1 to 1½ hundredweights
1 bag	=	1¼ to 1½ hundredweights
1 bale (Mocha)	=	2 to 2½ hundredweights
1 tierce	=	5 to 7 hundredweights

* also termed a robin.

Table 5.25 Cocoa Weights   [37, 40]

1 bag	=	1 hundredweight
1 cask	=	1 ¼ hundredweights

Table 5.26 Plums Weights   [40]

1 carton	=	9 pounds
¼ box	≈	20 pounds

Table 5.27 Prunes Weights   [37, 40]

1 barrel	=	1 to 3 hundredweights
1 puncheon	=	10 hundredweights

Table 5.28 Currants Weights   [37]

1 bag	=	4 hundredweights
1 caroteel	=	5 to 9 hundredweights
1 butt	=	15 to 20 hundredweights

Table 5.29 Raisins Weights   [37, 40]

1 box (Malaga)	=	22 pounds
1 drum (Valencia)	=	24 pounds
1 box (Valencia)	=	30 to 40 pounds
1 cask (Malaga)	=	1 hundredweight
1 cask (Turkey)	=	2 ½ hundredweights

Table 5.30 Figs Weights [37]

1 tapnet	=	20 pounds
1 drum (Turkey)	=	24 pounds
1 frail (Faro)	=	32 pounds
1 frail (Malaga)	=	56 pounds
1 sort	=	3 frails

Table 5.31 Almonds Weights [37, 40]

1 box (Jordan)	=	25 pounds
1 basket	=	1¼ to 1½ hundredweights
1 seron	=	1¼ to 2 hundredweights
1 bag	=	3 hundredweights

Table 5.32 Cloves Weights [40]

1 matt	=	80 pounds
1 chest	=	200 pounds

Table 5.33 Ginger Weights [37, 40]

1 jar (green ginger)	=	40 pounds
1 bag (East Indies)	=	1 hundredweight
1 bag (Jamaica)	=	1 hundredweight
1 bag (Barbados)	=	1¼ hundredweights

Table 5.34 Rice Weights [37]

1 bag (East Indies)	=	1½ hundredweights
1 cask (America)	=	6 hundredweights

Table 5.35 Cotton Wool Weights [37, 40]

1 bale (Brazilian)	=	220 pounds
1 bale (East Indian)	=	396 pounds
1 bale (USA)	=	477 pounds
1 bale (Egyptian)	=	719 pounds

Table 5.36 Cochineal Weights [37, 40]

1 pound	=	70,000 insects
1 seron	=	140 pounds
1 chest	=	168 pounds
1 bag	=	200 pounds

Table 5.37 Miscellaneous Commodities Weights [37, 40]

Aniseed	1 bag	3 - 4 hundredweights
Ballast	1 pig	56 pounds
Biscuits	1 bag	102 pounds
Bristles	1 cask	10 hundredweights
Camphor	1 box	1 hundredweight
Candles	1 barrel	120 pounds
Carraway seeds	1 bale	3 hundredweights
Cinnamon	1 bale	92½ pounds
Feathers	1 bale	1 hundredweight
Galls	1 sack	1½ hundredweights
Goats' hair	1 bag	2 - 4 hundredweights
Gum (Turkey)	1 chest	4 hundredweights
Gum Arabic (East Indies)	1 chest	6 hundredweights
Honey	1 gallon	12 pounds

[Table continued on next page]

Table 5.37 (contd) Miscellaneous Commodities Weights

Limestone	1 heap	=	5 tons
Mace	1 case	=	1½ hundredweights
Madder	1 cask	=	15 - 23 hundredweights
Magnesia	1 chest	=	1 hundredweight
Molasses	1 puncheon	=	10 - 12 hundredweights
Mustard	1 cask, small	=	9 - 18 pounds
	1 cask, large	=	18 - 36 pounds
Nutmegs	1 cask	=	200 pounds
Nuts (Barcelona)	1 bag	=	126 pounds
Pepper, black	1 bag	=	316 pounds
Pepper, white	1 bag	=	168 pounds
Quicksilver [mercury]	1 bottle	=	84 pounds
Rags (Hamburg)	1 bale	=	2¼ hundredweights
Rags (Mediterranean)	1 bale	=	4¼ - 5 hundredweights
Resin	1 barrel	=	2 hundredweights
Sago	1 bag	=	1 hundredweight
Salt	1 peck	=	14 pounds
	1 bushel	=	56 pounds
Shellac	1 chest	=	1 - 3 hundredweights
Soda	1 cask	=	3 - 4 hundredweights
Steel	1 faggot	=	120 pounds
Tallow	1 stone	=	8 pounds
	1 cask	≈	9 hundredweights
Tapioca	1 barrel	=	1¼ hundredweights
Tobacco	1 hogshead	=	12 - 18 hundredweights
Turpentine	1 barrel	=	2 - 2½ hundredweights
Vermilion	1 bag	=	50 pounds
Walnuts	1 bag	=	1 hundredweight

6. Money

This chapter examines various coins and monies of account used over the centuries, chiefly in England. For ease of reference, early mintings of mostly gold coins are listed alphabetically in Table 6.1. Initially each coin contained an amount of gold equal to its value, but from time to time the pieces were debased by adding other metals as alloys or their weights or values were altered with changing financial conditions. The majority of coins in this table were discontinued before or during the 19th Century. Table 6.1 shows the commonly used style of 6/8 (etc) to indicate six shillings and eight pence or 6s.8d. (etc). The / is an adaptation of the long s (often erroneously equated to f) used in printing and writing until the 19th Century. The / in 6/8 is merely an abbreviation for the first s in shilling or solidus (see later). In fact, the correct name for / is not slash, but solidus. It will be seen that a mark (13/4) was never minted as a coin, as explained below, although coins of half-a-mark were. Table 6.1 is followed by a chronological elaboration of the development of English coinage and currency. Table 6.2 lists coins that were in circulation during the 19th Century; many of these, apart from the gold coins, continued in use for much of the 20th Century.

Some crude indications of the changing values of money are offered in Tables 6.3 to 6.6, taken mainly from *Chronology* [ref. 27] published in 1826, and from a leaflet from the Royal Mint, published in 1972. These can be only crude as are most attempts to produce comparisons, because of the large number of variables which must be considered. Inflation cannot be measured simply by studying a range of probate inventories or by analysing the prices of bread or houses, the wages of labourers or the amount of coinage in circulation. Over the centuries, wages have not risen at the same rate as prices of goods and services, whilst the prices of different commodities such as grain, clothing, fuel, land and property have fluctuated by dissimilar amounts. Added to this are the quite different changes in standards of living and consumer expectations (eating habits, attitudes towards luxury items etc) of labourers compared with the gentry, and variations between rural and urban communities which, themselves, are not consistent across the country. Detailed studies (that of J E T Rogers fills seven volumes and most others are extremely complex) have attempted to provide indices and compare past values with those of today; Lionel Munby's pamphlet *How Much is that Worth?* [ref. 20], although not solving the problems, does highlight the difficulties more interestingly than most. Some money mentioned in the Bible is given in Table 6.8.

Table 6.1 Gold Coins Unique to pre-19th Century Mintings [10, 22]

1 angel	=	6/8 (from 1464); 7/6 (from 1526); 10/- (from 1550)
	=	2 angelets (from 1464)
1 crown *	=	5/- (from 1535)
1 crown-of-the-rose	=	4/6 (from 1526)
1 dollar	=	4/9 (from 1800)
1 florin	=	6/- (from 1344)
1 George noble	=	6/8 (from 1526)
1 guinea	=	20/- (from 1663); 21/- (from 1718)
1 helm (quarter-florin)	=	1/6 (from 1344)
1 leopard (half-florin)	=	3/- (from 1344)
1 noble (half-a-mark)	=	£⅓ = 6/8 (from 1344)
1 rose-noble	=	100 pence (from 1464)
1 ryal	=	10/- (from 1464); 15/- (from 1553)
1 sovereign	=	20/- (from 1489 and later); 22/6 (from 1526); 30/- (from 1550)
1 testoon †	=	12 pence (from 1489)
1 thistle crown	=	4/- (from 1604)
1 unite ‡	=	20/- (from 1604)

Note: some of the above coins are illustrated in Figure 7.1 on page 84.

* crowns were later (1551) minted in silver, see the following text.

† minted only in silver.

‡ nicknamed a laurel from 1604 and a broad from 1649.

A silver penny introduced at the end of the 8th Century replaced the silver (and later, copper) sceatta, which had itself replaced the 7th Century gold thrymsa - the first native coins of England. Prior to then Roman coins such as gold aurei, silver denarii and bronze alloy sesterii and asses had been used. The penny was on a similar standard to the silver denier then circulating in most of Western Europe and contained a denarius' (Latin for penny) worth of silver by weight.

When Alfred the Great (871-899) had driven the Danes out of London in 886 large numbers of silver pennies were struck bearing his portrait on the obverse. Halfpennies in silver were first minted at the same time, although half and quarter pennies were also improvised by individuals who cut pennies into halves and quarters; such cut pieces were accepted as currency. During the reign of Aethelred II (978-1016), the round penny and halfpenny were being produced at 75 mints across Britain, including some owned by episcopal authorities.

A gold penny, the first post-Conquest gold coin, was struck in 1257 for Henry III (1216-72) at a value of 20 silver pennies. A gross or groat of four pennies was introduced in 1279 by Edward I (1272-1307) but this was not a success and was discontinued for over seventy years. Silver halfpennies and farthings were issued regularly from this time by the Royal Mint within the Tower of London. Edward's silver pennies circulated widely in Western Europe.

In January 1344, under Edward III (1327-77) and almost 100 years behind the rest of Europe, a permanent gold coinage was introduced in England comprising florences or florins, valued at 6/-, and half-florins and quarter-florins called leopards and helms. In August 1344 the gold noble, valued at 6/8, (80 pence, half-a-mark or one-third of a pound), was issued and the florin, leopard and helm withdrawn. A coin to represent one mark (160 pence, 13/4, or two-thirds of a pound) was never minted although considerable accounting was undertaken in marks. Accordingly the mark is an example of "money of account", with some lawyers charging 6/8 well into the 20th Century. A similar example is the 21/-guinea, used as a unit of account, particularly for works of art, even long after the 1971 decimalization.

Monetary reforms in 1346 and 1351, necessary partly because of the influx from Europe of imitation silver pennies, reduced the weight, but not face value, of gold and silver coins. New gold nobles, half-nobles, and quarter-nobles were struck and silver groats (4d) and half-groats (2d) were produced, modelled on the failed groat of Edward I. Only silver pennies and halfpennies were struck at provincial mints, whilst the Tower Mint in London struck also gold coins.

From 1412, under Henry IV (1399-1414), weights of coins were again reduced but their face values were unaltered. The episcopal mints continued to produce lower-denomination silver pieces. However, in 1464 during Edward IV's first reign (1461-70), three new gold coins were introduced, the rose noble valued at 100 pence, displaying the Yorkist rose, the ryal or rial valued at 120 pence (10/-), struck for less than a decade at some provincial mints, and the angel (showing St

Michael slaying a dragon), having the same value as the earlier noble of 6/8. The ryal and the Rose noble soon became synonymous. From Henry VI's restoration in 1470, angels and half-angels were the only gold coins minted. Silver groats, half-groats, pennies, halfpennies and farthings continued to be produced.

A new coinage of Henry VII (1485-1509) in 1489 introduced a gold double-ryal of 20/- (termed a sovereign, as it depicted Henry in his sovereign's robes), a gold ryal showing the Tudor rose, not the York rose on the ryal of 1464, an angel, a half-angel and in 1504 a new (short-lived) silver testoon containing a solidarius' (Latin for shilling) worth of silver, with new designs for groats and pennies.

Apart from a new design of silver farthing, Henry VIII (1509-47) initially made no changes to previous coinage. However, financial problems in 1523 required debasement of gold and silver and a new coinage, increasing the value of the sovereign to 22/6 and the gold angel to 7/6; a gold coin equivalent to the French ecu, the crown-of-the-rose valued at 4/6, was introduced in 1526 but superseded almost immediately by a 5/- crown-of-double-rose. A new gold George noble (portraying St George slaying a dragon), of 6/8 was struck in 1526; but this and the crown-of-the-rose did not last long, the latter being replaced in 1545 by a gold crown of 5/- when a gold half-sovereign was also minted. The silver groat was redesigned, and again in 1544, when the coinage was further debased and the testoon re-introduced; the half-groat and penny were also redesigned.

Under Edward VI (1547-53) the silver testoon was termed shilling, thus ending the period when the shilling, like the mark, had been only a "money of account". New designs for the gold half-, quarter- and halfquarter-sovereign were brought in during 1549 and 1550. After 1550, besides the sovereign valued at 30/-, new designs were struck in gold of a sovereign of 20/-, a half-sovereign, a crown and a half-crown. The gold angel, now valued at 10/- but following earlier designs, was also minted. In 1551 a crown and a half-crown in silver were struck for the first time and new issues of fine silver shillings, sixpences and threepences (also minted for the first time) were produced. This was the last reign in which a silver farthing was produced. It may be noted that the fourth centenary of the silver crown was marked in 1951 by the issue by George VI of a crown valued at 5/-.

During Mary I's reign (1553-54) designs of the gold 30/- sovereign, 15/- ryal, angel and half-angel and the silver groat, half-groat and penny were improved. Only the angel and half-angel (angelet) were minted in gold during the joint reigns of Philip and Mary (1554-58) but silver shillings, half-shillings, groats, half-groats and pennies were produced, the groats and lower denominations bearing only Mary's portrait. No silver crowns were minted from 1553 to 1558.

Elizabeth I (1558-1603) withdrew most of the base money and a new series of gold pounds, half-pounds, crowns and half-crowns was minted, in addition to the previous gold sovereigns, ryals and angels. The silver crown and half-crown were re-introduced, and two new silver coins, the three-halfpence and three-farthings, were added to the now familiar shilling, sixpence, groat, threepence, half-groat and penny. The 3d, 1½d, and ¾d displayed a rose behind the Queen's head to distinguish them from the similarly-sized 4d, 2d, and 1d. Some coins showed the year of issue. The technology of milled coinage, in contrast to previously struck or hammered coins, became available during Elizabeth's reign, but was not fully employed in the production of official coins for another hundred years. Nonetheless, the gold half-pound, crown and half-crown and the silver shilling, sixpence, groat, threepence and half-groat were milled at this time.

Initially James I (1603-25) issued gold coins similar to those at the end of the previous reign. The silver 1/-, 6d, 2d, and 1d displayed their values in numerals; the ½d resembled that of Elizabeth I. In 1604 he issued a 4/- thistle crown, a 30/- rose ryal (replacing the 30/- sovereign), a 15/- spur ryal, and in reduced fineness a 20/- unite (called a laurel because of the wreath over the King's head), a 10/- double-crown, a 5/- Britain crown (in addition to the 10/- angel and the 5/ angelet) and a 2/6 half-crown; the thistle design was carried also on the silver half-groat and lower denominations. The values of all gold and silver coins were raised by 10% in 1611 but reduced again in 1619. The first copper pieces in English coinage were regally authorized in 1613 and copper farthings, really tokens rather than true coins, were privately manufactured by Lord Harington, it being thought undignified for the Royal Mint to issue copper coinage.

Charles I (1625-49) produced the gold angel valued at 10/- and a triple-unite of 60/-, while gold unites, half-unites and quarter-unites of 20/-, 10/- and 5/- were also minted with these values shown in Roman numerals (see Table 1.2) behind Charles's head. The silver crown and half-crown did not show their value but the silver shilling, sixpence, groat, threepence, half-groat and penny did. No silver farthings were minted after this reign. Copper farthing tokens continued to be made by other grantees. Hammered and milled coins were produced at this time.

During the Civil War the Tower Mint was controlled by Oliver Cromwell but many provincial mints continued to issue coins of varying denominations supporting the Royalist cause. For example, the Oxford mint produced gold triple-unites, unites, half-unites, and silver pounds, half-pounds, crowns, half-crowns, shillings, sixpences, groats, threepences, half-groats and pennies; the Shrewsbury mint manufactured silver coins from pounds to shillings but only the triple-unite in gold; at Bristol gold unites and half-unites and silver coins from half-crowns to half-groats were minted. Following Charles I's execution in 1649, coins were minted for the Commonwealth government with legends solely in English for the only time in the history of English coinage.

At the Restoration of Charles II (1660-85) some excellent quality gold coins were produced including a unite (nicknamed a *broad*) of 20/-, a double-crown or half-unite of 10/- and a crown or quarter-unite of 5/-. Only the half-crown, groat, threepence, half-groat and penny were minted in silver, the value being shown on the obverse behind the monarch's head. In 1662 hammered coins were replaced entirely by milled coins. From 1663, a new gold guinea valued at 20/-, named after African Guinea whence the gold was mined, and five-guinea, two-guinea and half-guinea pieces were minted. The date of issue was shown on the reverse side of coins for the first time. Silver crowns, half-crowns, shillings, sixpences, fourpences, threepences, twopences and pennies were issued, the values being marked in Cs on the fourpences and coins of lower denominations. The regnal year was also inscribed on the edge of the gold five-guinea, the silver crown and silver half-crown, to discourage clipping. In 1672 official copper halfpenny and farthing coins were minted containing their value of copper in each coin. The figure of Britannia appeared for the first time on British coins and faced left. To discourage forgery in 1684 tin farthings were issued with a copper plug.

The reign of James II (1685-88) introduced the tradition, which continues to this day, of successive monarchs being displayed alternately facing to the left and right. Charles II had faced right, James II was to the left. The values of the lower denomination silver coins were shown in Roman numerals, as Cs were obviously inappropriate. Halfpennies and farthings were minted only in tin.

Little changed regarding coinage during William and Mary's joint reign (1689-94; William reigned alone after Mary's death until 1702) although in 1694 the halfpenny and farthing were minted in copper and the lion of Nassau was included on most gold and silver coins. The values on the silver groats, threepences, twopences and pennies were shown as crowned numerals on the reverse of each coin. The hammered money still in circulation was being so badly clipped that in 1694 a tax to pay for some new coinage was imposed on all marriages (and births and burials) - see Chapmans Records Cameo: *Pre-1841 Censuses and Population Listings in the British Isles*; mints were re-opened at Bristol, Chester, Exeter, Norwich and York to cope with production until 1698. Sixpences were nicknamed *simons* at this time. Distribution of the new coins began in 1695 as the hammered coinage was withdrawn from circulation.

The now established gold and silver coins continued to be minted during the reign of Queen Anne (1702-14) although the designs were changed; the lion of Nassau disappeared and after the 1707 Act of Union with Scotland, the arms of both countries were conjoined. Vigo was displayed on some gold and silver coins to indicate their minting from captured bullion from Spanish ships in Vigo Bay in 1702. Only the farthing was produced in copper and this solely in 1714.

On George I's accession, a new gold quarter-guinea was produced and in 1718, under the influence of Sir Isaac Newton, Master of the Mint, the value of a guinea was fixed at 21/-. The appearance of roses and plumes on silver coins indicated that the metal had been mined in England or Wales. The silver shillings of 1723-26 bore WCC to identify mines owned by the Welsh Copper Company.

From 1729, during the reign of George II (1727-60), the silver 4d, 3d, 2d and 1d minted annually with a crowned numeral were reserved solely for Maundy distribution. Other gold and silver coins, similar to those of previous reigns, continued to be produced. During the 18th and well into the 19th Century the scarcity of low denomination coins was obviated by tradesmen issuing copper, and some silver, tokens. These were used to purchase goods or services at a particular establishment or were redeemable, in theory, by the tradesman for regal coinage at the value shown on each token. To a lesser extent these tokens had been issued in previous centuries; as in most cases the tradesman's name and place of operation is shown, they can be useful adjuncts in genealogical research.

Whilst George III was on the throne (1760-1820) no five-guinea or two-guinea pieces were minted for circulation although the gold guinea and half-guinea were widely issued. A gold third-guinea (seven shillings) was produced from 1797 to 1813 but the quarter-guinea was minted only in 1762. The guinea and half-guinea from 1787 to 1799 were nicknamed *spade guineas* because of the shape of the royal shield used on the reverse during those years. The silver shilling was issued only in 1763 and 1787 and the silver sixpence only in 1787, as a result of a silver shortage in the lead-up to the Napoleonic Wars. Nevertheless, there had been a large issue of 3d and 4d in 1762 and 1763 to satisfy the need for small change.

Counterfeit coins were a problem at this time, guineas being produced in brass and lightly gilded. In 1789 false coiners were referring to silver crowns, half-crowns, shillings and sixpences as *bulls, half-bulls, bobs* and *tanners*, the counterfeit coins being manufactured in *flats* (base metals).

Because of the shortage of silver coins, Spanish dollars, counter-marked with the bust of George III were officially valued at 4/9 and put into circulation in 1800. In addition the Bank of England in 1804 issued silver bank dollars valued at 5/- and in 1811 silver token coins of 3/- and 1/6. Whilst not distributed from the Royal Mint this token coinage was legal tender. The 5/- dollars caused the silver crowns also to be nicknamed *dollars*, well into the 20th Century. Copper halfpennies and farthings were minted from 1770 to 1775. In 1797 copper pennies were minted, each containing exactly one ounce of copper, about a pennyworth. Tuppenny (two-penny) coins containing exactly two ounces of copper were issued also in 1797, having been minted under contract in Birmingham, and similar halfpennies and farthings were issued in 1799. The 1d and 2d coins were nicknamed *cartwheels* because of the broad band around their edges and their heaviness. They were used by tradesmen as weights for scales. The 2d copper coins proved too bulky for personal use and were never minted again; lighter copper coins in 1806 and 1807 were in the penny, halfpenny and farthing denominations only. The value of the sovereign was fixed at 20/- in 1816 and as a consequence a gold sovereign valued at 20/- and a half-sovereign of 10/- were issued in 1817; the sovereign and crown bore the now-famous St George and Dragon designed by Benedetto Pistrucci on their reverses [hence *george* for sovereign] while the half-sovereign, half-crown, shilling and sixpence had a shield of arms. By 1811 a new Royal Mint had been constructed at Tower Hill where it began minting in 1816 and remained for the next 150 years.

In 1823, under George IV (1820-30), a gold double-sovereign was minted together with the sovereign and half-sovereign. The designs of the silver crown, half-crown, shilling and sixpence were changed twice during this reign with a lion shown standing on a crown on the reverse of the shilling from 1825 and sixpence from 1826. Britannia faces right from 1821 for the first time on the copper farthing and from 1825 on the penny and halfpenny.

No silver crowns were issued for circulation by William IV (1830-37) but the silver groat was re-introduced in 1836. On the 1/- and 6d the values ONE SHILLING and SIX PENCE are shown on two lines, a feature which remained on the 6d until 1910.

During Queen Victoria's reign (1837-1901) gold coins of five-pounds, two-pounds, guinea, sovereign and half-sovereign continued to be minted, as did silver crowns, half-crowns, shillings, sixpences, groats, threepences and three-halfpennies. In 1847 the crown was minted with Gothic lettering and nicknamed accordingly. The silver florin was minted in 1849 as one-tenth of a pound in an attempt, which failed at that time, to decimalize British currency. As the inscription Dei Gratia was omitted, it was nicknamed a *Godless florin*. In 1851 the florin was issued with Gothic lettering and the production of 2/6 was suspended until 1863 to encourage the use of the new coin. It was to be another 120 years before currency decimalization became a reality. A silver double-florin was issued from 1887 but withdrawn in 1890 as it was confused with the crown. The silver groat had become nicknamed a *joey* after Joseph Hume the politician who promoted savings banks, and who found it convenient for paying the 8d London cab fare; after his death in 1855 the groat ceased to be minted in Britain from 1856 for circulation here, although it continued to be produced for use in some British colonies into the 20th Century. A new silver threepence was minted from 1845. Pennies, halfpennies, farthings and half-farthings in copper were produced with the year of issue generally on the obverse, particularly at the start of Victoria's reign. Copper third-farthings and quarter-farthings were minted but used mostly in British colonies. From 1860 the penny, halfpenny and farthing were issued in token value in a bronze alloy and the year of issue returned to the reverse. (Some vulgar names which have been applied over the years to British money are on the inside of the back cover.)

To conserve gold during the First World War, paper pound and ten-shilling notes were issued and no gold half-sovereigns were minted for circulation after 1915 and no gold sovereigns after 1917, although some colonial mints continued to issue them until 1932. Mintings of gold and fine silver coins in a variety of denominations for collectors and investors, not intended for circulation but nevertheless mostly legal tender, became increasingly popular in the latter quarter of the century. In 1920, also resulting from the War, the silver content of all silver coins was reduced from 92.5% to 50% and in 1947 to zero when a cupro-nickel alloy was henceforth used for all "silver" coins. The Iver Heath Mint in Buckinghamshire supplemented the production of Royal Mint coins from 1940. The half-crown was demonetized on 1 January 1970 (ceased to be legal tender after 31 December 1969) in preparation for decimalization of the currency in 1971 on 15 February. £sd, derived from LSD, (Librae, Solidi, Denarii), Pounds, Shillings, Pence, in Latin, which had been used for centuries became £p, pounds and new (decimal) pence; £1.00 = 100p. Comparisons between pre-1971 and decimal currency are given in Chapter 7, Table 7.11. Commemorative crowns valued at 5/- or 25p in cupro-nickel and also fine silver were issued for events such as Elizabeth II's coronation in 1953, the death of Churchill in 1965 and the Queen Mother's 90th Birthday in 1990. In similar metals, commemorative £2 coins were minted occasionally from 1986. Pound coins were minted regularly from 1983; the pound had been nicknamed a *quid* since the 17th Century but in the early years of the 20th Century the vulgar term *nicker* emerged, whence ten shillings became *half-a-nicker*. In equally common parlance, the horse-racing and gambling fraternity nicknamed £25, £100, £500, £100,000 and a million pounds respectively *a pony, a ton, a monkey, a plum* and *a marigold*.

New fifty-pence and new twenty-pence coins, both seven-sided in "silver", were circulated from 1969 and 1982 respectively, although at the latter issue the word "new" was omitted from this and all later mintings of English coins. The florin was minted until 1967 and continued in circulation until 1993 although a "silver" new (decimal) ten-pence coin of identical size and weight was minted from 1968; this size of ten-pence coin was also withdrawn from circulation in 1993. The shilling suffered the same fate as the florin and was last minted in 1966; a new "silver" five-pence, having the same size and weight as the shilling, was circulated from 1968. Further new designs and smaller sizes of five and ten pence coins were introduced in 1990 and 1992 respectively and the former sizes and designs withdrawn. The sixpence was not minted after 1967; for nearly ten years after decimalization it circulated as 2½p but was demonetized on 1 July 1980. In 1937 the silver threepence (threepenny piece), nicknamed *Tom, Trip and Go*, was replaced by a twelve-sided brass threepenny or thruppeny bit. The silver 3d was not minted after 1945. Both the silver threpenny pieces and the brass threpenny bits, and also the penny (1d), were demonetized on 1 September 1971. A new (decimal) bronze penny (1p) was introduced in 1971, as was a new bronze two (new) pence coin. The bronze halfpenny, for most of its life termed a ha'penny, was demonetized on 1 August 1969. A new (decimal) half-pence coin was minted from 1971 but was demonetized on 1 January 1985 when the denomination of even the new halfpenny was abolished altogether. No bronze farthings were minted after 1956 and the farthing was demonetized on 1 January 1961. Until 1970 silver 4d, 3d, 2d and 1d, and from 1971 silver 4p, 3p, 2p, and 1p continued to be minted as Maundy Money for distribution by the reigning monarch every year on Maundy Thursday. The Mint in London produced its final coin, a gold sovereign, in November 1975; the new Royal Mint at Llantrisant, near Cardiff in South Wales, had already begun production of new coins in 1968 in preparation for decimalization.

Table 6.2 Sterling Coins used during the 19th Century [22, 36]

Copper or Bronze		
1 farthing (¼d)	=	2 half-farthings
1 ha'penny (½d)	=	2 farthings
1 penny (1d)	=	2 ha'pennies
Silver		
1 three-ha'pence (1½d)	=	3 ha'pennies
1 threppence (3d)	=	3 pennies
1 groat (4d)	=	4 pennies
1 sixpence (6d)	=	6 pennies
1 shilling (1s or 1/-)	=	12 pennies
1 florin	=	2 shillings (2/-)
1 half-crown	=	2 shillings & sixpence (2/6)
1 three-shillings	=	3 shillings (3/-)
1 double-florin	=	4 shillings (4/-)
1 dollar	=	5 shillings (5/-)
1 crown	=	5 shillings (5/-)
Gold		
1 quarter-guinea	=	5 shillings & threepence (5/3)
1 third-guinea	=	7 shillings (7/-)
1 half-sovereign	=	10 shillings (10/-)
1 half-guinea	=	10 shillings & sixpence (10/6)
1 sovereign	=	1 pound (£1)
	=	20 shillings (20/-)
	=	240 pence (240d)
1 guinea	=	21 shillings (£1-1s)
1 double-sovereign	=	2 pounds (£2)
1 five-pounds	=	5 pounds (£5)

Table 6.3 Some Financial Allowances and Salaries [31, 32]

Year	Allowance or Salary
900	King Alfred bequeathed to each of his daughters £100.
1221	Joan, eldest daughter of King John, upon her marriage with Alexander, King of Scotland, had a dowry of £1000 per annum.
1278	Edward I, gave with his daughter Joan, contracted to the son of the King of the Romans, 10,000 Marks sterling (to be restored if he died before her).
1314	Elizabeth, consort of Robert Bruce, King of Scotland, being imprisoned in England, was allowed for herself and family 20 shillings a week.
1350	Joan of Oxford, nurse to the Black Prince, had a pension of £10 per annum; Maud Plumpton, a rocker, had a pension of 10 Marks per annum. Pensions allowed by the King to the Cardinals (great officers of the Pope) but retained by the English Court, were at the most 50 Marks per annum.
1351	Workmen were to take their wages in wheat at the rate of 10d per bushel; a master carpenter, mason or tiler were allowed by the day 3d, their journeymen 2d, and their servants or boys 1½d.
1402	The salary of a Lord Chief Justice of the King's Bench was £40 per annum.
1408	The salary of the Lord Chief Justice of the Common Pleas was 55 Marks per annum.
1500	An admiral, if a knight, had while at sea 4s per day; if a baron 6s.8d per day; if an earl 13s.4d per day.
1545	The Lord Chief Justice of the King's Bench had an addition of £30 to his salary.
	Each Justice of the same Bench and Common Pleas had an addition of £20.

Note: a rocker (1350) is a cradle-rocker.

Table 6.4 Wages of Husbandmen - per day [27]

Year	Wage	Year	Wage
1568	4d	1698	8d
1620	4½d	1716	9d
1632	6d	1740	10d
1647	10d	1760	1/-
1662	6d	1788	1/4
1688	8d		

Table 6.5 Prices for a Quartern Loaf of Bread [27]

Date	Price	Date	Price
1754	4d	Jan 1801	1/11
1757	7½d	July 1810	1/5
Mar 1800	1/5	July 1823	10d

Note: see the note to Table 5.10.

A Quartern loaf was vulgarly termed a georgy.

Table 6.6 Living costs, compared with those in 1796 [27]

Year	Comparison
1066	seven times cheaper
1381	six times cheaper
1403	ten times cheaper
1440	four times cheaper
1498	three-and-a-half times cheaper
1560	near five times cheaper

Table 6.7 Purchasing Power of the Shilling

Year	Cost	Item
930	One shilling	One sheep
1300	One shilling	A pair of shoes
1300	Seven shillings	An acre of land
1500	Four shillings	An artisan's weekly wage
1650	One shilling	A tooth extraction
1750	One shilling	A skilled worker's daily wage
1750	One shilling	Four miles' travel in winter in a stage coach
1965	One shilling	A large bar of chocolate

Table 6.8 Biblical Coins   [33]

quadrans	(Mark Ch.12,v.42)	2 mites (leptons)
assyrium (penny)	(Matthew Ch.10,v.27)	4 quadrantes
denarius (drachma)	(Matthew Ch.20,v.2)	16 asses
bekah (didrachma)	(Exodus Ch.38,v.26)	2 drachma
shekel (tetradrachma	(Genesis Ch.23,v.16)	2 bekah
or silverling)	(Matthew Ch.17,v.27)	1 slater
mineh *	(Luke Ch.19,v.13)	50 shekels
talent	(II Kings Ch.5,v.22)	60 minehs

The quadrans and assyrium are copper, the remainder are silver coins.

* termed a mina in New Testament times, when = 30 shekels.

7. Metric Measures & Equivalents

A metric system, in which all measurements should be multiplied or divided by ten, first proposed by a priest of Lyon in 1670 and encouraged by French revolutionaries, was approved by Louis XVI and finally introduced in 1795. Before this, the various regions in France had an even greater diversity of measuring units than given in the Chapters 1 to 6 above. The basic unit chosen was a mètre, then calculated as a ten-millionth part of the distance of a line running on the earth's surface through Paris, from the North Pole to the Equator. Sub-units of the mètre are décimètre, centimètre, etc (with Latin prefixes) while multiple-units are the décamètre, hectomètre and kilomètre, etc (with Greek prefixes), as identified in Table 1.15. A standard mètre bar, made of platinum-iridium alloy, was kept in Paris. (The metre, later having the grave accent dropped, was defined in 1960 in terms of optical wavelengths in vacuum of radiation from atoms of krypton-86; today it is realised through the wavelength of the 633 nm radiation from an iodine-stabilized helium-neon laser).

From the metre as a unit of length, the French developed the are as the unit of area (equal to 100 square metres, ie, a square decametre), the stère as the unit of cubic measure (also losing its accent, and equal to a cubic metre), the litre as the unit of capacity (equal to one-thousandth of a stere) and the gram (originally spelled gramme) as the unit of mass of one cubic centimetre (one-thousandth of a litre) of water at its maximum density, four degrees Centigrade or Celsius (4°C). As the French tended to use centimetres for their day-to-day activities, in preference to metres, and also picked the second for the standard measure of time, this choice of units of measurement was termed the centimetre-gram-second (CGS) system; this became accepted in many parts of the world, although those countries with a strong British influence retained Imperial units.

Towards the end of the 19th Century more importance was placed on the metre and the kilogram (the weight of one litre of water) as fundamental units and hence the metre-kilogram-second (MKS) system was adopted under the influence of the Conférénce Générale des Poids et des Mésures (CGPM). The International Electrotechnical Commission officially adopted the MKS system in 1935 and incorporated electromagnetic units into it. In 1950 following the efforts of Giorgi, the ampere as a unit of electric current was formally accepted as a fourth basic unit, resulting in the MKSA system, sometimes termed Giorgi's system. At its 10th meeting in 1954 the CGPM included the kelvin as the unit of temperature

(273 K = 0°C = 32°F) and the candela as the unit of luminous intensity to create the Système International d'Unités (SI) series of metric units, formalised at its 11th meeting in 1960. This was extended in 1964 at the 12th CGPM meeting to include radionuclides. A summary of today's SI base units confirmed in 1991, is shown in Table 7.1; other units are derived from these, although many aspects of the daily lives of people in the British Isles, the United States and elsewhere are still closely related to many of the units of measurement tabulated in Chapters 1 to 6. Some comparisons between units most recently used in the British Isles of linear, square and cubic measure and of measures of capacity and weight and of currency, and metric units and decimal currency are given in Tables 7.2 to 7.11.

Table 7.1 SI Base Units   [47]

Quantity	Unit & Symbol	Definition
Time	second (s)	The duration of 9 192 631 770 periods of the radiation corresponding to the transition between the two hyperfine levels of the ground state of the caesium-133 atom.
Length	metre (m)	Length of the path travelled by light in vacuum during a time interval of 1/299 792 458 of a second.
Mass	kilogram (kg)	The unit of mass; it is equal to the mass of the international prototype * of the kilogram.
Electric current	ampere (A)	That constant current which, if maintained in two straight parallel conductors of infinite length, of negligible circular cross-section, and placed 1 metre apart in vacuum, would produce between these conductors a force equal to 2×10^{-7} newton per metre of length.

[Table continued on next page]

Table 7.1 (contd) SI Base Units

Quantity	Unit & Symbol	Definition
Thermodynamic temperature	kelvin (K)	The unit of thermodynamic temperature is the fraction 1/273.16 of the thermodynamic temperature of the triple point of water.
Amount of substance	mole (mol)	The amount of substance of a system which contains as many elementary entities as there are atoms in 0.012 kilogram of carbon-12.
Luminous intensity	candela (cd)	The luminous intensity, in a given direction, of a source that emits monochromatic radiation of frequency 540×10^{12} hertz and that has a radiant intensity in that direction of (1/683) watt per steradian.

* the International prototype is made of platinum-iridium and is kept at the International Bureau of Weights and Measures, Sèvres, France; the British copy (No.18) is kept at the National Physical Laboratory, Teddington, England.

SI supplementary units are the radian (the plane angle between two radii of a circle which cut off on the circumference an arc equal in length to the radius) and the steradian (the solid angle which, having its vertex in the centre of a sphere, cuts off an area of the surface of the sphere equal to that of a square with sides of length equal to the radius of the sphere).

Quantities such as area (square metre) and volume (cubic metre) are termed derived units, some of which have special names such as the newton, the unit of force (kilogram metres per second squared: $m\ kg\ s^{-2}$), and the joule, the unit of energy (newton metres: $m^2\ kg\ s^{-2}$).

Table 7.2 Imperial to Metric Conversion (Length)

Imperial	Metric
1 inch	25.4 millimetres
1 foot	0.3048 metre
1 yard	0.9144 metre
1 furlong	201.168 metres
1 mile	1.60993 kilometres

Table 7.3 Imperial to Metric Conversion (Area)

Imperial	Metric
1 square inch	6.4516 square centimetres
1 square foot	9.2903 square decimetres
1 square yard	0.8361 square metre
1 acre	0.4047 hectare
1 square mile	259.00 hectares

Table 7.4 Imperial to Metric Conversion (Volume)

Imperial	Metric
1 cubic inch	16.387 cubic centimetres
1 cubic foot	0.0283 cubic metre
1 cubic yard	0.7645 cubic metre

Table 7.5 Imperial to Metric Conversion (Capacity)

Imperial	Metric
1 gill	0.142 litre
1 pint	0.568 litre
1 quart	1.136 litres
1 gallon	4.546 litres
1 peck	9.092 litres
1 bushel	36.37 litres

Table 7.6 Imperial to Metric Conversion (Apothecaries' Capacity)

Imperial	Metric
1 minim	0.059 millilitre
1 fluid scruple	1.184 millilitres
1 fluid drachm	3.552 millilitres
1 fluid ounce	28.412 millilitres
1 pint	0.568 litre

Table 7.7 Imperial to Metric Conversion (Troy Weight)

Imperial	Metric
1 grain	0.0648 gram
1 pennyweight	1.5552 grams
1 Troy ounce	31.103 grams
1 Troy pound	0.3732 kilogram

Table 7.8 Imperial to Metric Conversion (Apothecaries' Weight)

Imperial	Metric
1 grain	0.0648 gram
1 scruple	1.296 grams
1 drachm	3.888 grams
1 ounce	31.103 grams

Table 7.9 Imperial to Metric Conversion (Avoirdupois Weight)

Imperial	Metric
1 grain	0.0648 gram
1 dram	1.772 grams
1 ounce	28.350 grams
1 pound	0.453 kilogram
1 stone	6.350 kilograms
1 quarter	12.70 kilograms
1 hundredweight	50.80 kilograms
1 ton	1.016 tonnes

Note: a megagram or 1000 kilograms is also termed a tonne or metric ton and, formerly, a millier.

Table 7.10 Metric to Imperial Conversion (All Measures)

Measure	Metric	Imperial
Length	1 metre	39.37 inches
Area	1 square metre	10.7639 square feet 1.1960 square yards
Volume	1 cubic centimetre	0.0610 cubic inch
	1 cubic metre	35.3147 cubic feet 1.3079 cubic yards
Capacity	1 litre	1.7598 pints
Mass or Weight	1 gram	15.432 Troy grains 0.03215 Troy ounce 0.2572 Apothecaries' drachm 0.7716 Troy scruple 0.5644 Avoirdupois dram
	1 kilogram	2.2046 Avoirdupois pounds

Table 7.11 British Pre-decimal Currency and Decimal Equivalents

Pre-Decimal Value	Decimal Value from 1971
sixpence (6d)	two-&-a-half pence (2½p) *
shilling (1/-)	five pence (5p)
florin (2/-)	ten pence (10p)
half-a-crown (2/6)	twelve-&-a-half pence (12½p) *
five shillings (5/-)	twenty-five pence (25p)
ten shillings (10/-)	fifty pence (50p or £0.50)
one pound (£1.0s.0d.)	one pound (£1.00)
one guinea (£1.1s. or 1 Gn)	one pound & five pence (£1.05)

* the decimal half pence was demonetized on 1 January 1985 (see Chapter 6).

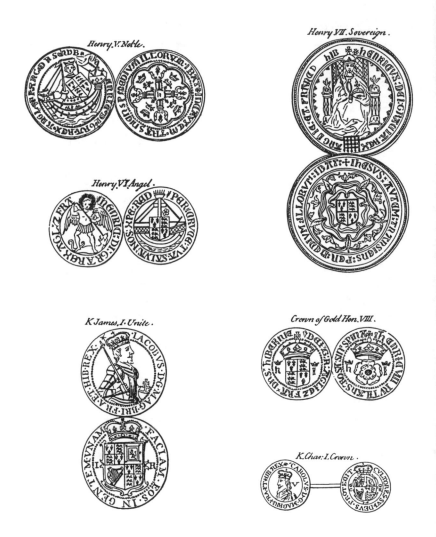

Fig 7.1 Illustrations of some coins first published by Bishop Fleetwood in 1707 [ref. 10].
(see Table 6.1 and the text of Chapter 6).

References and Bibliography

Besides a number of Parliamentary Papers and Acts of Parliament, several sources have been consulted in the preparation of this booklet. Further details than can be accommodated in this compact handbook can be found in the following. The first 30 works are by identifiable authors in alphabetical order; the remainder, collective, works are listed chronologically by date of publication.

1. George B Airy (Sir). *Philosophical Transactions*. Royal Society. Pt 3, p 17. 1857.

2. Charles Arbuthnot. *Tables of Ancient Coins, Weights and Measures etc*. 1727.

3. Algernon E Berriman. *Historical Metrology*. 1953.

4. P H Bigg & Pamela Anderton. *Nature*. Vol 200 p 730. 1963.

5. P H Bigg & Pamela Anderton. *British Journal of Applied Physics*. Vol 15, pp 291-300. 1964.

6. Henry J Chaney. *Our Weights and Measures*. 1897.

7. Henry W Chisholm. *On the Science of Weighing & Measuring*. 1877.

8. Robin D Connor. *The Weights and Measures of England*. 1987.

9. Wordsworth Donisthorpe. *A System of Measure of Length, Area, etc*. 1895.

10.William Fleetwood (Bishop). *Chronicon Preciosum - English Money etc*. 1707.

11.Richard T Glazebrook (Sir). *Dictionary of Applied Physics*, Vol 3. 1922-23.

12.John Greaves. *Origins and Antiquity of Our English Weights and Measures*. 2nd edn. 1745.

13.Charles E Guillaume. *Proceedings*. Physical Society. Vol 32 p 374 et seq. 1920.

14.Hubert Hall & Frieda J Nicholas. *Camden Miscellany*. Vol 15. 1929.

15.Charles Hutton. *A Course of Mathematics etc*. Rev edn. 1833.

16.Patrick Kelly. *Metrology. 1816*.

17.Benjamin Longwith. *Observations on Dr Arbuthnot's Dissertation*. 1747.

18.W H Miller. *Philosophical Transactions*. Royal Society. Vol 146 p 753. 1856.

19.Theodor Mommsen. *Hermes: Zeitschrift für Classische Philologie*. pp 152-156. 1888.

20.Lionel Munby. *How Much is that Worth ?* 1989.

21.Edward Nicholson. *The Story of our Weights and Measures* 1901.

22.Edward Nicholson. *Men and Measures*. 1912.

23.John Richardson. *Local Historian's Encyclopaedia*. 1983.

24.Rogers Ruding (Rev). *Annals of the Coinage of Britain*. 1807-1840.

25.J E Sears. *Cantor Lectures*. Royal Society of Arts. 1923.

26.John Taylor. *Battle of the Standards*. 1864.

27.Thomas Tegg. *Chronology, or the Historian's Companion*. 4th Edn. 1826.

28.Charles M Watson (Sir). *British Weights & Measures*. 1910.

29.Paul & B R Withers. *British Coin Weights, a Corpus etc*. 1994.

30.Ronald E Zupko. *Dictionary of English Weights and Measures*. 1968.

31.*Pocket Companion & Annual Accompt-Book for MDCCLXXXVIII*. 1788.

32.*Walkers Pronouncing Dictionary*. 1826.

33.*Companion to the Bible*. 1831.

34.*The Athenaeum*. Nos 2603-2606, pp 338, 371, 403, 433. 15 Sep - 6 Oct 1877.

35.*Notes & Queries*. 6th series. Vol 11 p 206. Jan - Jun 1885.

36.*Business Encyclopaedia and Legal Adviser*. 1913.

37.*Pears Cyclopaedia*; (Office Compendium). 1924.

38.*Fowler's Mechanics' and Machinists' Pocket Book*. 1933.

39.*Chambers's Technical Dictionary*. 1940.

40.*Nuttall's Table Book*. c1950.

41.*Schoolboy's Pocket Book*. 1951.

42.*Odhams Dictionary of the English Language*. 1956.

43.*Collins Civil Engineers Diary*. 1963.

44.*Junior Pears Encyclopaedia*. 1981.

45.*Whitaker's Almanack*. 1983.

46.*Every Boy's Handbook*. 1983.

47.*Units of Measurement*. National Physical Laboratory. 1991.

48.*International Vocabulary of Basic and General Terms in Metrology*. ISO, Geneva. 1993.

Index to Tables

Measures are given in normal type, commodities in italic.